GOVERNMENT PROCEDURES AND OPERATIONS

NATIONAL MEDIATION BOARD: ASSESSMENT, STRATEGIC PLAN, AND FAQS

GOVERNMENT PROCEDURES AND OPERATIONS

Additional books in this series can be found on Nova's website under the Series tab.

Additional e-books in this series can be found on Nova's website under the e-book tab.

GOVERNMENT PROCEDURES AND OPERATIONS

NATIONAL MEDIATION BOARD: ASSESSMENT, STRATEGIC PLAN, AND FAQS

TINA JIMENEZ
EDITOR

New York

Library of Congress Cataloging-in-Publication Data

ISBN: 978-1-63485-993-6

Published by Nova Science Publishers, Inc. † New York

CONTENTS

PREFACE

The National Mediation Board (NMB) was established under the Railway Labor Act to facilitate labor relations for railroads and airlines by mediating and arbitrating labor disputes and overseeing union elections. The FAA Modernization and Reform Act of 2012 included a provision for United States Government Accountability Office (GAO) to evaluate NMB programs and activities every 2 years. GAO's first report under this provision, issued in December 2013, included seven recommendations for NMB based on assessments of policies and processes in several management and program areas. This book examines the extent to which NMB has implemented recommendations made by GAO in December 2013, and incorporated key procurement practices.

In: National Mediation Board
Editor: Tina Jimenez
ISBN: 978-1-63485-993-6

Chapter 1

NATIONAL MEDIATION BOARD: PROGRESS MADE ON SOME GAO RECOMMENDATIONS TO STRENGTHEN OPERATIONS, BUT KEY CONTROLS CONTINUE TO BE NEEDED*

United States Government Accountability Office

ABBREVIATIONS

DHS	Department of Homeland Security
FedRAMP	Federal Risk and Authorization Management Program
Fiscal Service	Department of the Treasury's Bureau of the Fiscal Service
FISMA (2002)	Federal Information Security Management Act of 2002
FISMA (2014)	Federal Information Security Modernization Act of 2014
GPRA	Government Performance and Results Act of 1993
GPRAMA	GPRA Modernization Act of 2010
NMB	National Mediation Board
NRAB	National Railroad Adjustment Board

* This is an edited, reformatted and augmented version of The United States Government Accountability Office publication, GAO-16-240, dated February 2016.

OMB	Office of Management and Budget
OPM	Office of Personnel Management
RLA	Railway Labor Act

WHY GAO DID THIS STUDY

NMB was established under the Railway Labor Act to facilitate labor relations for railroads and airlines by mediating and arbitrating labor disputes and overseeing union elections. The FAA Modernization and Reform Act of 2012 included a provision for GAO to evaluate NMB programs and activities every 2 years. GAO's first report under this provision, issued in December 2013, included seven recommendations for NMB based on assessments of policies and processes in several management and program areas.

This second report examines the extent to which NMB has 1) implemented recommendations made by GAO in December 2013, and 2) incorporated key procurement practices. GAO reviewed relevant federal laws, regulations, and NMB documents, such as its strategic and workforce plans; and contracting data for fiscal years 2014-2015; and interviewed NMB officials.

WHAT GAO RECOMMENDS

GAO recommends that NMB develop and implement written policies and processes to reflect its current procurement environment. NMB agreed with the recommendation and indicated it would take steps to implement it.

WHAT GAO FOUND

The National Mediation Board (NMB) has made some progress in addressing the seven recommendations GAO made in December 2013; however, additional actions are needed to fully implement those recommendations and strengthen operations (see table). Without full implementation, NMB lacks reasonable assurance that its limited resources are effectively targeted and may be missing opportunities to improve performance and mitigate risks in program and management areas.

NMB's Actions in Response to GAO's December 2013 Recommendations

GAO's 2013 recommendations	NMB's actions	Additional actions needed to address recommendations
Develop a formal strategic planning process	Published a strategic plan in fiscal year 2014.	Develop formal written policies and procedures governing its planning process.
Develop performance goals and measures	Developed new performance goals.	Ensure performance goals meetall guidelines for federal performance management.
Develop and implement formal mechanism to resolve audit findings/recommendations	Developed a written process to resolve financial statement audit findings and recommendations.	Expand the written process to address all audits.
Develop and fully implementan information security program	Moved to a cloud computing environment and outsourced certain functions.	Develop and implement policies and procedures and assess third-party providers' implementation of security requirements.
Establish aninformation privacy program	Designated an official responsible for privacy.	Assess impact on privacy and issue notices about personally identifiable information NMB uses and shares.
Develop a strategic workforce plan	Completed a plan that addressed most required elements.	Formally include stakeholders in planning process and evaluate workforce planning and other human capital efforts.
Collect and analyze rail grievance arbitration data	Collected data for some cases on types of grievances.	Collect data on all cases and analyze.

Source: GAO analysis of NMB documents and interviews with officials. | GAO-16-240.

NMB is following some key procurement practices that GAO has identified in prior work. However, NMB has not developed and implemented written policies and processes—consistent with internal control standards and best practice— that reflect its new interagency agreement with the Department of the Treasury for the performance of certain procurement functions. Without this documentation NMB cannot ensure the use of consistent processes in its new procurement environment.

* * *

February 12, 2016

The Honorable John Thune
Chairman

The Honorable Bill Nelson
Ranking Member
Committee on Commerce, Science, and Transportation
United States Senate

The Honorable Lamar Alexander
Chairman

The Honorable Patty Murray
Ranking Member
Committee on Health, Education, Labor, and Pensions
United States Senate

The Honorable Bill Shuster
Chairman

The Honorable Peter A. DeFazio
Ranking Member
Committee on Transportation and Infrastructure
House of Representatives

The National Mediation Board (NMB), created by a 1934 amendment to the Railway Labor Act (RLA), oversees union elections and provides mediation, arbitration, and other services to resolve railroad and airline labor disputes, including resolving disputes over issues such as working conditions, rates of pay, and union representation.[1] Currently, NMB delivers services to management and labor unions at 150 commercial airlines and over 500 railroads. NMB has 51 full-time staff positions and had a fiscal year 2015 appropriation of approximately $13 million.

The FAA Modernization and Reform Act of 2012 further amended the RLA and included a provision for us to evaluate and audit the programs, operations, and activities of NMB every 2 years.[2] We issued our first report in December

2013, which reviewed agency planning and controls related to several management and program areas and included seven recommendations to address deficiencies in these areas (see table 1).[3]

Table 1. GAO's December 2013 Report Recommendations to the National Mediation Board (NMB)

Management/Program Areas	Recommendation
Strategic planning	Develop a formal strategic planning process to fully implement key required elements of strategic planning, including a formal process to obtain congressional and stakeholder input.
Performance management	Develop, and include in its performance plan, performance goals and measures that contain required elements to demonstrate results.
Auditor findings and recommendations	Develop and implement a formal mechanism to ensure the prompt resolution of findings and recommendations by independent auditors, including clearly assigning responsibility for this follow-up to agency management.
Information security	Develop and fully implement key components of an information security program in accordance with the Federal Information Security Management Act of 2002.
Information privacy	Establish a privacy program that includes conducting privacy impact assessments and issuing system of record notices for systems that contain personally identifiable information.
Workforce planning	Develop a strategic workforceplan that (1) involves input from top management, employees, and other stakeholders; (2) identifies critical skills and competencies needed by NMB; (3) identifies strategies, such as training, to address any gaps; and (4) provides for cost-effective evaluations of these strategic workforce planning efforts. This plan should also address succession for the significant proportion of NMB staff and senior managers who are eligible to retire in the next few years.

Table 1. (Continued)

Management/Program Areas	Recommendation
Rail grievance arbitration	In order to betterinform its decisions about managing the rail grievance arbitration process,including addressing the backlog of cases, NMB should collect and analyze data on the types of grievances filed, and their disposition. NMB should use these data to improve the efficiency of the arbitration process and consider, as part of this effort, whether to establish fees for arbitration services. If NMB determines that the establishment of fees would improve the efficiency of the arbitration process, it should impose such fees or seek legislative authority to do so, as necessary.

Source: GAO-14-5 | GAO-16-240.

In our December 2013 report we also found that NMB did not follow procurement policies and procedures it had in place at that time. The agency developed a checklist for taking the required steps in the procurement process that responded to those findings prior to the issuance of the 2013 report. We did not, therefore, make any recommendations in that area at that time.

In addition, we found that the Office of Management and Budget (OMB) and Office of Personnel Management (OPM) provided limited budgetary and human capital oversight of NMB, the agency did not have mechanisms to monitor its operations and programs, and independent auditors' findings were not being addressed. As a result, we suggested that Congress consider authorizing an appropriate federal agency's Office of Inspector General to provide independent audit and investigative oversight of NMB.

This is the second review of NMB and this report examines the extent to which NMB:

1. has implemented each of our December 2013 recommendations, and
2. has incorporated key procurement practices.

To address our objectives, we reviewed relevant federal laws and regulations. We also assessed NMB documents related to strategic planning, performance management, information security, information privacy, workforce planning, and procurement using Standards for Internal Control in the Federal Government,[4] provisions of the Federal Information Security Modernization Act (FISMA) of 2014,[5] Privacy Act of 1974, E-Government Act of 2002, the Government Performance and Results Act of 1993 as updated by the GPRA Modernization Act of 2010 (GPRAMA), guidance developed by OMB and in the National Institute of Standards and Technology Special Publication 800-53 Revision 4, as well as criteria on strategic workforce planning[6] and best practices in procurement developed by GAO in prior work.[7]

We analyzed NMB's contract actions for fiscal years 2014 and 2015 using data provided by the Department of the Treasury's Bureau of the Fiscal Service.[8] We assessed the reliability of these data and information from NMB's fiscal year 2013 through 2015 financial statement audit reports[9] by interviewing knowledgeable officials and reviewing relevant documents. We determined that these data were sufficiently reliable for our purposes.

We interviewed NMB officials and current board members. We also interviewed key stakeholders who were interviewed for the December 2013 report, including representatives from rail and air management and labor groups. The results of these interviews are not generalizable to all NMB stakeholders.[10] Further, we interviewed officials at OMB and OPM to determine how these agencies provide oversight and guidance to NMB. For additional details, see appendix I.

We conducted this performance audit from April 2015 to February 2016 in accordance with generally accepted government auditing standards.

Those standards require that we plan and perform the audit to obtain sufficient, appropriate evidence to provide a reasonable basis for our findings and conclusions based on our audit objectives. We believe that the evidence obtained provides a reasonable basis for our findings and conclusions based on our audit objectives.

BACKGROUND

NMB's Organization and Mission Background

NMB is headed by a three-member board, with each member appointed by the President and confirmed by the Senate for a term of 3 years.[11] Day-to-day administration of the agency is provided by NMB's General Counsel within the Office of Legal Affairs and the Chief of Staff (see fig. 1). NMB does not have an office of inspector general to provide independent audit and investigative oversight.

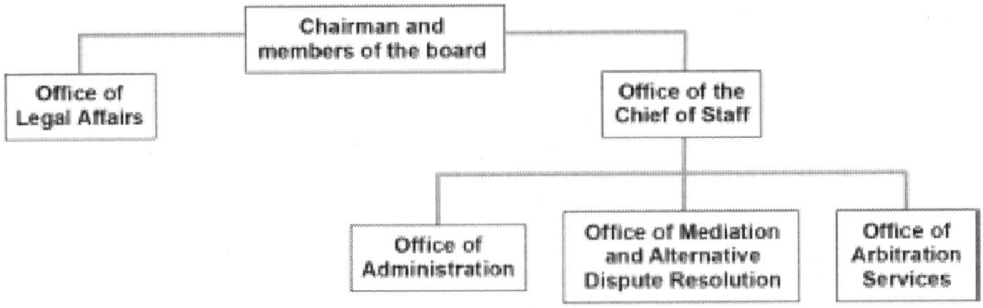

Figure 1. Organization of the National Mediation Board.

According to NMB, its overall mission is to provide for the independence of air and rail carriers and employees in matters of self-organization, avoid interruption to commerce conducted through the operation of those carriers, and administer statutory adjustment boards as well as develop complementary strategies to resolve disputes. To fulfill its mission, NMB has three program areas:

- Representation: Unions are selected for the purposes of collective bargaining through secret-ballot elections conducted by NMB. If there is a question concerning representation of a specific craft or class,[12] NMB is charged with resolving the representation dispute through its Office of Legal Affairs, and has the sole jurisdiction to decide these disputes.[13]
- Mediation and Alternative Dispute Resolution: The RLA provides mediation to help resolve disputes that can occur between management and labor during collective bargaining negotiations.[14] When rail or air carriers and unions cannot reach agreement on the terms of a new or revised collective bargaining agreement—such as working conditions or rates of pay—either party can apply for NMB's mediation services to resolve their differences or NMB may impose mediation if it finds that resolving the dispute is in the public's interest. NMB also offers grievance mediation to parties as an alternative way to resolve disputes filed for grievance arbitration.
- Arbitration: The RLA also offers grievance arbitration to help resolve disagreements between carriers and unions over how to interpret and

apply provisions of existing collective bargaining agreements.[15] For example, employees may file grievances if they believe they were wrongfully fired or disciplined in violation of the agreement. If the carrier and the employee cannot resolve the grievance, the RLA permits either of these parties to refer the dispute to arbitration before an adjustment board.[16] The adjustment board consists of a carrier representative, a union representative, and a neutral arbitrator provided by NMB. In this capacity, the arbitrator is called upon to break a tie. NMB does not directly provide arbitration services, but rather maintains a list of registered arbitrators from which the parties can select someone to review and decide their case. In the airline industry, the parties pay the costs of arbitration. In the railroad industry, however, consistent with the requirements of the RLA, NMB pays the fee and travel expenses of the arbitrator.

NMB Has Made Progress, but Has Not Yet Fully Implemented GAO's 2013 Recommendations

NMB has made some progress in implementing each of the seven recommendations we made in December 2013.

Developing a Strategic Planning Process

> GAO 2013 Recommendation: NMB should develop a formal strategic planning process to fully implement key required elements of strategic planning, including a formal process to obtain congressional and stakeholder input.
>
> Source: GAO-14-5 | GAO-16-240.

In our December 2013 report, we found that NMB lacked a formal strategic planning process and officials confirmed that they did not have a systematic mechanism for involving congressional and other stakeholders in this process. We concluded that without a robust process, NMB lacked assurance that its limited resources were effectively targeted toward its highest priorities.

In this review, we found that NMB has implemented a strategic planning process but has not formalized it through written policies and procedures. In fiscal year 2014, NMB developed and published a strategic plan covering fiscal years 2014 through 2019, which we determined was largely consistent with OMB guidance[17] on implementing the GPRA Modernization Act of 2010 (GPRAMA).[18] NMB officials told us they used a strategic planning process soliciting input from staff in NMB program areas as well as from external stakeholders and Congress.[19] Five of the seven external stakeholder groups that we interviewed said they commented on a draft of the strategic plan or discussed aspects of it during regular meetings with the agency, and all reported being satisfied with their overall communication with NMB.

However, the agency has not developed a written policy or set of procedures outlining its strategic planning process. Federal internal control standards call for agencies to document the policies and procedures necessary to achieve their objectives, including strategic planning.[20] Specifically, agencies should (1) establish policies and procedures to ensure that management directives are carried out and (2) appropriately document transactions and other significant events, and ensure that those records are properly managed, maintained, and available for examination. Further, through these policies and procedures, agency management can define responsibilities, assign key roles, and delegate authority.

Meeting these requirements may be particularly important for NMB. NMB officials said there was little need for preparing written documentation of the strategic planning process, such as a standard operating procedure, because it was simple and would be easy to replicate in the future. Officials also said, because the agency is small, with 51 full-time positions, its staff frequently communicate informally, limiting the need for written procedures. However, three of NMB's five senior managers, including the Chief of Staff and General Counsel, are eligible to retire, as are many other employees, increasing the risk of the agency losing institutional knowledge should they do so. Moreover, because the agency is small, some staff members have multiple responsibilities, increasing the magnitude of knowledge loss when an individual staff member leaves the agency.

Establishing Performance Goals and Measures

GAO 2013 Recommendation: NMB should develop, and include in its performance plan, performance goals and measures that contain required elements to demonstrate results.

Source: GAO-14-5 | GAO-16-240.

In our December 2013 report, we found that NMB was not meeting OMB guidance to implement GPRAMA requirements for annual performance planning and reporting. Specifically, the agency's performance goals were not objective, quantifiable, and measurable—as required by GPRAMA[21]— and did not have targets and a time period over which to measure performance—as recommended by OMB guidance implementing GPRAMA.[22] Without meeting this federal guidance, we concluded that the agency was not positioned to track and publicly report progress or results in its program areas.

In this review, we found that NMB has developed new performance goals. However, of the 19 goals in its fiscal year 2016 performance plan, one goal specified a target, another specified a timeframe; but none followed all elements of OMB guidance for implementing GPRAMA.[23] Several NMB officials told us that it is difficult for the agency to design performance goals because some outcomes are out of its control, such as how long it takes parties to reach agreement through mediation. Many federal agencies also set measurable performance goals for outcomes that include external factors outside of their direct control. Our prior work has shown that there are a number of strategies that federal agencies can use to reduce the influence of external factors on agencies' measures.[24] OMB officials told us NMB could seek assistance from them to refine its performance goals or could partner with another agency that has a strong performance management department.

Resolving Auditor Findings and Recommendations

GAO 2013 Recommendation: NMB should develop and implement a formal mechanism to ensure the prompt resolution of findings and recommendations by independent auditors, including clearly assigning responsibility for this follow-up to agency management.

Source: GAO-14-5 | GAO-16-240

In our December 2013 report, we found that NMB was following most key practices for financial accountability and control, but had an outstanding significant deficiency from its fiscal year 2012 financial statement audit and did not have a mechanism for ensuring prompt resolution of audit findings.[25] As a result, we concluded that some recommendations made by auditors to improve the agency's internal controls or operations may not have been addressed.

In this review, we found that while NMB in fiscal year 2015 resolved the significant deficiency identified in its 2012 financial statement audit,[26] it does not have a formal mechanism to promptly resolve all audit findings consistent with federal internal control standards.[27] Specifically, while NMB drafted a financial audit standard operating procedure in 2014, it does not cover the agency's response to findings from non-financial audits. The agency has also not addressed two recommendations made in previous auditors' management letters that accompanied NMB's financial audit reports.[28] One of those recommendations was made as a result of the fiscal year 2014 audit and the other recommendation was related to a discrepancy that has been unresolved since 1995.[29] In its fiscal year 2015 response, NMB indicated that the only management official with knowledge of the long-term discrepancy had retired and the agency would work to resolve the discrepancy through its financial management system.

Ensuring Information Security and Privacy

GAO 2013 Recommendations:

- Develop and fully implement key components of an information security program in accordance with the Federal Information Security Management Act.
- Establish a privacy program that includes conducting privacy impact assessments and issuing system of records notices for systems that contain personally identifiable information.

Source: GAO-14-5 | GAO-16-240.

In our December 2013 report, we found that NMB had not fully implemented key practices for information security and privacy. Without implementation of these key practices, we concluded that NMB had increased risks that the confidentiality, integrity, and availability of its information would be compromised and it had limited assurance that the personal information it collected and used was adequately protected.[30]

In this review, we found that NMB has fully transitioned its network infrastructure and records management system into a cloud computing environment as a result of federal initiatives aimed at improving, among other things, the federal government's operational efficiencies and overall IT security posture.[31] NMB also fully transitioned its financial systems to third-party service providers. Specifically, NMB relies on other agencies' systems, such as the Department of the Interior, for payroll, personnel, and human resources services, and the Department of the Treasury's Bureau of the Fiscal Service for a full range of accounting services, including hosting its financial management system.

In addition, NMB has begun to take steps to improve its information security program. Specifically, NMB developed a policy for managing agency information, documents, and records. The agency has also drafted procedures for its new enterprise network[32] that include provisions for access and identity control, configuration management, planning, contingency monitoring, and audits. Further, it has developed a procedure for handling cyber incidents. Finally, it has an agreement in place with the Bureau of the Fiscal Service to, among other things, conduct a security assessment of its enterprise network.

However, NMB has not fully implemented most key information security and privacy practices. (For additional details, see appendix II.) For example, the agency does not have policies and procedures in place for its information security program, including those for the oversight of third-party providers—entities that provide or manage information systems that support NMB operations. In addition, NMB has not conducted the required assessments of its third-party providers to ensure their systems are in compliance with the Federal Information Security Modernization Act (FISMA) of 2014.[33] FISMA requires federal agencies to develop, document, and implement an agency-wide information security program to protect the information and information systems that support the operations and assets of the agency, including those provided or managed by another agency, contractor, or other source.

Moreover, NMB has not assessed whether its third-party providers' systems were in compliance with the Privacy Act of 1974 and E-Government Act of 2002, which describe, among other things, agency responsibilities with regard to protecting personally identifiable information.[34]

NMB officials said the agency is taking steps to address its remaining information security and privacy issues. For example, because the agency's new enterprise network is now a cloud-based system, NMB plans to use the Federal

Risk and Authorization Management Program (FedRAMP),[35] to the extent possible, to guide the development of its agency-wide policies and procedures, including how it will oversee its third-party providers and ensure they are in compliance with FISMA. In addition, NMB reached out to OMB in September 2015, and NMB officials said they have tried reaching out to the Department of Homeland Security (DHS) to ensure NMB is doing what is required to meet annual FISMA reporting requirements.[36] NMB officials said they have been receiving information on FISMA from OMB, but not from DHS.[37]

Further, NMB officials said they are working on drafting information security program and privacy policies and procedures. They said that finalizing the information security policies and procedures will assist the agency in completing all of its required reviews in the future.

Developing a Strategic Workforce Plan

GAO 2013 Recommendation: NMB should develop a strategic workforce plan that (1) involves input from top management, employees, and other stakeholders; (2) identifies critical skills and competencies needed by NMB; (3) identifies strategies, such as training, to address any gaps; and (4) provides for cost-effective evaluations of these strategic workforce planning efforts. This plan should also (5) address succession for the significant proportion of NMB staff and senior managers who are eligible to retire in the next few years.

Source: GAO-14-5 | GAO-16-240.

In our December 2013 report, we found that NMB's human capital program was not guided by a strategic workforce plan. Without workforce planning, a key internal control,[38] we concluded that agency management could not ensure that skill needs would be continually assessed and that the agency would be able to obtain and maintain a workforce with the skills necessary to achieve organizational goals. Without a plan, the agency could not monitor and evaluate the results of its workforce planning efforts, including whether those efforts contributed to the agency accomplishing its strategic goals.[39]

Table 2. Extent to Which the National Mediation Board (NMB) Is Following Key Practices Related to GAO's December 2013 Workforce Planning Recommendation

Practice[a]	Extent NMB is following[b]	Examples of NMB's Implementation
Develop a strategic workforce plan that involves input from top management, employees, and other stakeholders.	Partially following	NMB officials told us the agency developed its workforce plan through a collaborative, agency-wide process, but they did not formally solicit feedback from stakeholders onthe plan and the plan did not specifically call for staff and stakeholder involvement. However, members of NMB's advisory group said they provided input to NMB on workforce decisions such as training and the hiring of key staff.
Develop a strategic workforce plan that identifies critical skills and competencies needed by NMB.	Following	NMB identified critical skills and competencies in its workforce plan.
Develop a strategic workforce plan that identifies strategies, such as training, to address any gaps.	Following	NMB has programs in place to provide training for staff, and has identified several strategies for recruiting a diverse workforce.
Develop a strategic workforce plan that provides for cost-effective evaluations of these strategic workforce planning efforts.	Minimally Following	NMB's workforce and succession plan did not address themonitoring and evaluation of its workforce planning efforts, and the performance goals in its strategic plan related to human capital do not meet all guidance.
Develop a strategic workforce plan that addresses succession for the significant proportion of NMB staff and senior managers who are eligible to retire in the next few years.	Following	NMB's workforce and succession plan evaluated the risk of vacancy of each position and provided narrative on the expected identification of replacement staff.

Source: GAO analysis of NMB documents and interviews with NMB officials. | GAO-16-240.

[a] These key practices were developed by GAO in GAO, Human Capital: Key Principles for Effective Strategic Workforce Planning, GAO-04-39 (Washington, D.C.: Dec. 11, 2003).

[b] We assessed whether NMB is following key practices (NMB is taking appropriate actions and has a formal plan, policy, or other document), partially following (is taking some actions but does not have a formal plan or policy and/or some additional steps must be taken to consider this practice implemented), or minimally following (NMB is taking little or no action to address this particular practice).

In this review, we found NMB in October 2014 completed a strategic workforce plan that at least partially addressed four of the five practices from our December 2013 recommendation (see table 2).[40]

While members of one of NMB's advisory groups said they provided input on some of the agency's workforce decisions, our prior work suggests that formally including stakeholders in the workforce planning process can help the agency develop ways to streamline processes and improve human capital strategies.[41] In addition, NMB's performance goals, including those related to human capital, do not meet federal guidance. Without performance goals that meet guidance or the inclusion of other monitoring and evaluation efforts in its workforce and succession plan, the agency is not positioned to measure the outcomes of its human capital strategies or evaluate whether these strategies helped it accomplish its goals.

Managing Rail Grievance Arbitration

GAO 2013 Recommendation: In order to better inform its decisions about managing the rail grievance arbitration process, including addressing the backlog of cases, NMB should collect and analyze data on the types of grievances filed, and their disposition. NMB should use these data to improve the efficiency of the arbitration process and consider, as part of this effort, whether to establish fees for arbitration services. If NMB determines that the establishment of fees would improve the efficiency of the arbitration process, it should impose such fees or seek legislative authority to do so, as necessary.

Source: GAO-14-5 | GAO-16-240.

In our December 2013 report, we found that NMB was struggling to efficiently manage grievance cases in the rail industry and it lacked data on the types of grievances filed to more efficiently manage the process. As a result, we concluded that if NMB did not address this demand on its limited resources, it could face a growing backlog of arbitration cases.

In this review, we found that NMB is collecting data on the type of grievances filed for arbitration in some, but not all cases. An NMB official said part of the reason the agency is not collecting complete data on grievance types is because it does not have access to all cases. NMB reviews all grievances filed for arbitration by either a railroad or union and then forwards them to one of three types of adjustment boards—the National Railroad Adjustment Board (NRAB), a Public Law Board, or a Special Board of Adjustment.[42] NMB is able to track information on the type of grievances filed for arbitration by the Public Law Boards and Special Boards of Adjustment because NMB requires parties to code their grievance type when they file their request for these boards.[43] Parties filing grievances with NRAB, however, are not required by NMB to code their grievance type, an NMB official said, because NRAB is an independent organization that sets its own procedures and NMB cannot require that grievance codes be included in requests for arbitration filed with NRAB. However, NMB may be able to obtain that information because NRAB officials told us they track information on grievance type and are willing to share this information with NMB.

Even with data on types of grievances filed for all cases, it is not clear the extent to which NMB would analyze them to address the arbitration backlog. One program official said that NMB does not have a systematic way to identify cases that may be good candidates for some type of alternative to arbitration, such as grievance mediation, because staff cannot easily access case information in a way that makes it readily available for analysis.[44] Analysis of these cases continues to be largely a manual process that takes significant staff resources, he said. According to an NMB information technologist, in the past, the agency has primarily relied on staff to sort and analyze these data. However, the agency's new arbitration case management system, which it upgraded in November 2015, should be able to produce by spring 2016 standard electronic data reports that would facilitate this analysis. Until those reports are available, it appears NMB will have limited ability to analyze data that might help it reduce its arbitration backlog, which, according to NMB, continues to grow.

NMB HAS NOT ESTABLISHED PROCUREMENT POLICIES AND PROCESSES THAT REFLECT ITS NEW PROCUREMENT ENVIRONMENT

NMB is following key procurement practices in 2 of 3 areas that our prior work on assessing the acquisition function at federal agencies identified as promoting agencies' efficient, effective, and accountable procurement functions—organizational alignment and leadership; and knowledge and information management.[45] NMB, however, has not developed policies and processes—a third area our prior work identified—that reflect its new procurement interagency agreement. After the retirement of its only contracting officer in January 2014, NMB entered into an interagency agreement with the Department of the Treasury's Bureau of the Fiscal Service (Fiscal Service) for provision of certain procurement functions that NMB had previously handled in-house.

In this new environment, NMB is continuing to align its procurement function with its mission and ensure adequate resources to meet its procurement needs, a key practice to facilitate efficient and effective management of acquisition activities. Its Office of Administration is at an organizational level comparable to other key mission offices, such as the Office of Mediation and Alternative Dispute Resolution and the Office of Arbitration. An NMB official told us that the agency also involves internal stakeholders in acquisition decisions, including determining procurement needs, reviewing existing contracts before automatically renewing them, and justifying purchase requests. In addition, the agency entered into the interagency agreement with the Fiscal Service in response to changes in its workforce (i.e., the retirement of its contracting officer). Further, to ensure NMB has a procurement workforce adequate to support the organization's needs, two staff are being trained as contracting officers because not having a contracting officer is a risk to the agency, the NMB official said.[46] In addition, six NMB staff were trained and certified as contracting officer representatives, who assist the contracting officer in providing administration of contract actions under the interagency agreement and evaluating performance.

NMB is also following a second key practice by establishing knowledge and information tools to help it make well-informed procurement decisions. NMB now has access to electronic data on purchase requests from the procurement and financial management systems administered by Fiscal Service. Fiscal Service also provides NMB with monthly billing reconciliations and weekly updates on the status of its contracts.[47] A NMB official said that the information received from Fiscal Service has helped the agency analyze and adjust its spending and, as a result, NMB has eliminated contracts for items it no longer needs, such as storage space, copiers, and periodical subscriptions.

However, NMB is not following an element of a third key practice—to have policies and processes in place consistent with internal control standards and best practice.[48] NMB has not developed written internal policies and processes that reflect its new interagency agreement procurement environment. The NMB procurement official said the agency does not have current policies and processes because some of the previous policies and procedures were lost in the transition which occurred when the previous contracting officer retired. As a result, the agency has had to recreate them, the official said. The agency's fiscal year 2014 to 2019 strategic plan (as amended in fiscal year 2015) called for procurement processes to be updated by the end of fiscal year 2014 in light of the new procurement environment. Developing and implementing written procurement policies and processes that reflect NMB's current procurement environment could help ensure its staff use consistent processes under this new environment.

CONCLUSIONS

Since we made our recommendations in December 2013, NMB has taken several positive steps in response, such as developing strategic and workforce plans and closing a long-standing deficiency in a financial statement audit. However, additional actions are needed to fully respond to those recommendations. For example, NMB's performance goals do not yet meet all federal guidance. As a result, the agency is not positioned to track and publicly report progress or results in its program areas. In the areas of strategic planning and information security and privacy, officials were not able to provide the written policies and procedures that guide their actions, consistent with standards for internal control. Without fully implementing these recommendations, NMB cannot ensure that its limited resources are effectively targeted toward its highest priorities. Moreover, it may be missing opportunities to improve performance and mitigate risks in its program and management areas. In addition, NMB has not developed written policies and procedures that reflect its new procurement environment under its interagency agreement. Without written policies and processes—as called for by internal control standards and best practice—NMB cannot ensure the use of consistent procurement processes.

We continue to believe, as suggested in our December 2013 report, that Congress should consider authorizing an appropriate federal agency's Office of Inspector General to provide independent audit and investigative oversight of NMB.

RECOMMENDATIONS FOR EXECUTIVE ACTION

We recommend that the Chairman of the National Mediation Board develop and implement written policies and processes to reflect the agency's current procurement environment.

AGENCY COMMENTS AND OUR EVALUATION

We provided a draft of this report to the National Mediation Board (NMB) for comment. The agency provided written comments, which are reproduced in their entirety in appendix III. We also shared a draft with the Office of Management and Budget (OMB) and Office of Personnel Management (OPM). Neither agency provided comments.

NMB commented that many of the areas we had concerns about are not under its direct control considering that NMB has entered into interagency agreements for certain services with the Department of the Interior and the Department of the Treasury's Bureau of the Fiscal Service (Fiscal Service). We continue to believe, however, that NMB must retain ultimate control and responsibility for all its programs and data, regardless of which agencies are to perform the services. For example, with regard to our findings related to information security, NMB commented that it will develop standard operating procedures for reviewing audits conducted by its third-party providers, but that it does not have the resources to conduct its own audits of those contracted agencies. Under FISMA, however, NMB is responsible for developing, documenting, and implementing a security program to protect its information systems and data, including those managed by another agency, contractor, or other source. We believe that developing procedures for reviewing audits conducted by third-party providers will be a positive step toward ensuring that NMB is conducting this required oversight.

NMB agreed with our recommendation to develop and implement policies and processes to reflect the agency's current procurement environment and indicated it is taking steps to do so. NMB also commented that because it does not manage all of its own procurements, its policies and processes would be largely subordinate to those of the Fiscal Service. However, because NMB's interagency agreement with the Fiscal Service for performance of certain procurement functions does not absolve NMB of its responsibility to develop policies and processes as called for by internal control standards and best practice, NMB must develop its own set of complementary policies and processes to ensure the agency meets its needs through efficient, effective, and accountable procurement functions.

In terms of its response to audits, NMB commented that all program audit findings have been addressed and that there are no outstanding issues related to any audits. While we recognized in the report that NMB resolved a long-standing, significant deficiency in its fiscal year 2015 financial statement audit, we disagree that all audit issues have been resolved. NMB needs to develop policies and procedures to address findings from all audits, not solely those reported in the financial statement audit report.

NMB also commented that some of our concerns appeared to be related to the agency's failure to sufficiently document its processes and that this was not necessarily an indication of noncompliance with any particular requirement. We agree that NMB has made strides in certain areas, such as developing strategic and workforce plans, but its actions are not in accordance with federal guidance or federal internal control standards in some areas. For example, in the areas of strategic planning, information security and privacy, and procurement, officials were not able to provide the written policies and procedures that guide their actions. We continue to believe it is important for NMB to create this documentation to ensure future consistency and success in its management and program areas.

Finally, NMB commented it had concerns that we continued to assert the agency did not adequately consult with its stakeholders even though we noted several times in the report that stakeholders told us they had input and were satisfied with their overall communication with the agency. Stakeholder groups did tell us they had good communication with NMB, particularly with regard to the agency's strategic planning. However, in the development of its workforce plan, NMB officials said that they did not specifically solicit stakeholder input, and the agency's workforce and succession plan does not address collecting and incorporating feedback from stakeholders. As our prior work suggests,[49] it will be important for NMB to formally include stakeholders in this process in the future because involving stakeholders can help the agency develop ways to streamline processes and improve human capital strategies.

We are sending copies of this report to the Chairman of NMB and appropriate congressional committees. In addition, the report is available at no charge on the GAO website at http://www.gao.gov.

If you or your staff have any questions about this report, please contact me at (202) 512-7215 or brownbarnesc@gao.gov. Contact points for our Offices of Congressional Relations and Public Affairs may be found on the last page of this report. GAO staff who made key contributions to this report are listed in appendix IV.

Cindy Brown Barnes
Director
Education, Workforce, and Income Security Issues

APPENDIX I: OBJECTIVES, SCOPE, AND METHODOLOGY

The FAA Modernization and Reform Act of 2012 included a provision for us to evaluate and audit the programs, operations, and activities of the National Mediation Board (NMB) every 2 years.[1] Our first report was issued in December 2013.[2] This is the second review of NMB and this report examines the extent to which NMB:

1. has implemented each of our December 2013 recommendations, and
2. has incorporated key procurement practices.

To address our research objectives, we reviewed key NMB documents and compared those documents with relevant federal laws, regulations, guidance, and related leading practices identified in our previous work (see table 3).

Table 3. GAO Comparison of Key National Mediation Board (NMB) Documents with Federal Laws, Guidance, and Leading Practices

Management area	NMB documents reviewed	Federal laws and guidance and previous GAO work
Strategic planning	NMB Strategic Plan, Fiscal Year 2014 through Fiscal Year 2019 (as amended in Fiscal Year 2015)	GPRA Modernization Act of 2010 (GPRAMA)[a]

Management area	NMB documents reviewed	Federal laws and guidance and previous GAO work
		Office of Budget and Management (OMB) CircularNo. A-11, Part 6 (2013)[b] Standards for Internal Control in the Federal Governmentc
Performance management	NMB Strategic Plan, Fiscal Year 2014 through Fiscal Year 2019 (as amended in Fiscal Year 2015) Fiscal Year 2016 Congressional Budget Submission	GPRAMA[a] OMB Circular No. A-11, Part 6 (2013 and 2014)[b, d] GAO prior work on performance measuremente
Resolution of audit findings and recommendations	Audit Standard Operating Procedure Fiscal Year 2013 Audit Report, Fiscal Year 2014 and 2015 Final Independent Auditors' Reports, and associated management letters	Standards for Internal Control in the Federal Governmentc
Information security and privacy	Fiscal Year 2015 Interagency Agreement and Fiscal Year 2015 Service Level Agreement between NMB and Department of the Interior Fiscal Year 2015 and Fiscal Year 2016 Interagency Service Agreements between NMB and Department of the Treasury Bureau of the Fiscal Service NMB information, documents, and records management policy and proposed draft revised policy Enterprise Cloud Standard Operating Procedures NMB's 2014 Draft System Security Plan for Enterprise Cloud (version 1.2) – May 2014 NMB Security Awareness Certificates Initial Internal Security Assessment for the NMB Enterprise Cloud – May 2014 NMB Preliminary Plan of Actions and Milestones NMB Cyber Incident Reporting Standard Operating Procedure NMB Continuity of Operations Plan – June 2011	Federal Information Security Modernization Act of2014f Privacy Act of 1974 E-Government Act of 2002 National Institute of Standards and Technology Special Publication 800-53, Revision 4 OMB Memos M-05-08 and M-15-01
Workforce planning	Workforce and Succession Plan - October 2014 NMB Strategic Plan, Fiscal Year 2014 through Fiscal Year 2019 (as amended in Fiscal Year 2015) Fiscal Year 2016 Congressional Budget Submission	GAO prior work on workforce planningg GPRAMA[a] OMB Circular No. A-11, Part 6 (2013 and 2014)[b, d]

Table 3. (Continued)

Management area	NMB documents reviewed	Federal laws and guidance and previous GAO work
Procurement	Fiscal Year 2015 and Fiscal Year 2016 Interagency Service Agreements between NMB and Department of the Treasury Bureau of the Fiscal Service Contract actions for Fiscal Year 2014 and Fiscal Year 2015[h]	Standards for Internal Control in the Federal Government[c] GAO prior work on procurement at federal agencies[i]

Source: GAO | GAO-16-240.

Notes:

[a] GPRA stands for the Government Performance and Results Act, Pub. L. No. 111-352, 124 Stat. 3866 (2011).

[b] Office of Management and Budget, Strategic Plans, Annual Performance Plans, Performance Reviews, and Annual Program Performance Reports, Circular No. A-11, Part 6 (July 2013).

[c] GAO, Standards for Internal Control in the Federal Government, GAO/AIMD-00-21.3.1 (Washington, D.C.: November 1999).

[d] Office of Management and Budget, Preparation and Submission of Strategic Plans, Annual Performance Plans, and Annual Performance Reports, Circular No. A-11, Part 6 (July 2014).

[e] GAO, Managing for Results: Measuring Program Results that Are Under Limited Federal Control, GAO/GGD-99-16 (Washington, D.C.: Dec. 11, 1998).

[f] The Federal Information Security Management Act of 2002 (FISMA 2002) established information security program and evaluation requirements for federal agencies. FISMA 2002 was largely superseded by the Federal Information Security Modernization Act of 2014 (FISMA 2014) that incorporates and continues the requirements of FISMA 2002 applicable to NMB.

[g] GAO, Human Capital: Key Principles for Effective Strategic Workforce Planning, GAO-04-39 (Washington, D.C.: Dec.11, 2003).

[h] For fiscal year 2015, we only looked at contract actions from October 1, 2014, through August 3, 2015,because that was the date the Bureau of the Fiscal Service responded to our data request..

[i] GAO, Framework for Assessing the Acquisition Function at Federal Agencies, GAO-05-218G (Washington, D.C.: September 2005).

We interviewed NMB officials and current board members. In addition, we interviewed key stakeholders who were interviewed for the December 2013 report, among others. Specifically, we interviewed representatives from key rail and air management and labor groups including Airlines for America, National Railway Labor Conference, AFL-CIO Transportation Trades Department and affiliated rail and air unions, and the International Brotherhood of Teamsters.

Further, we interviewed representatives from the National Association of Railroad Referees, an association representing railroad arbitrators; the Dunlop II Committee, an informal NMB advisory group; and the National Railroad Adjustment Board, which hears rail grievance arbitration cases. The results of these interviews are not generalizable to all NMB stakeholders.[3] Finally, we interviewed officials at the Office of Management and Budget and the Office of Personnel Management to determine how these agencies provide oversight and guidance to NMB.

In addition, we reviewed NMB procurement data. Specifically, we reviewed data provided by the Department of the Treasury's Bureau of the Fiscal Service on NMB's fiscal year 2014 and 2015 contract actions.[4] We assessed the reliability of data from the Bureau of the Fiscal Service and NMB's fiscal year 2013 through 2015 financial statement audit reports[5] by interviewing knowledgeable officials and reviewing relevant documents. We determined that these data were sufficiently reliable for our purposes.

We conducted this performance audit from April 2015 to February 2016 in accordance with generally accepted government auditing standards. Those standards require that we plan and perform the audit to obtain sufficient, appropriate evidence to provide a reasonable basis for our findings and conclusions based on our audit objectives. We believe that the evidence obtained provides a reasonable basis for our findings and conclusions based on our audit objectives.

Appendix II: Extent to Which the National Mediation Board (NMB) Is Following Key Practices for Information Security and Privacy

Practice	Extent NMB is following[a]	Example of NMB's status
Information Security Practices[b]		
Periodic risk assessments	Minimally following	NMB has not conducted risk assessments of its new enterprise network and financial management systems.
Risk-based policies and procedures	Partially following	NMB developed a policy for managing agency information, documents, and records in May 2013. In addition, it drafted procedures for its new

Appendix II: (Continued)

Practice	Extent NMB is following[a]	Example of NMB's status
		enterprise network that include provisions for access and identity control, configuration management, planning, contingency monitoring, and audits. However, NMB has not developed agency-wide policies and procedures that govern its information security program, including policies and proceduresfor the oversight of third-party providers.
System security plans	Partially following	NMB has drafted a security plan for its new enterprise network dated May 2014. However, NMB has not developed a security plan for its new financial management systems.
Security awareness training	Minimally following	NMB stated its staff was provided security awareness training during 2015. However, NMB did not provide evidence to support that all employees and contractors had received the training.
Periodic testing and evaluation at least annually	Partially following	NMB conducted an initial review of its new enterprise network in May 2014. NMB stated its new financial management systems were reviewed in September 2014. However, NMB was unable to provide evidence to support the review.
Remedial action process	Partially following	NMB has not established and documented a remedial action process for its information security control weaknesses. NMB has not formally documented and tracked its preliminary plan of actions for its new enterprise network and

Practice	Extent NMB is following[a]	Example of NMB's status
		has not included required attributes, such as milestones and scheduled completion dates. In addition, NMB has not yet begun formally documenting and tracking any information security control weaknesses which have been identified through other reviews (e.g., GAO).
Security incident procedures	Partially following	NMB has developed a procedure for handling cyber incidents. However, there are no indicators of date, review and approval. In addition, the procedure does not include required actions, such as mitigating risks associated with incidents before substantial damage is done, and notifying and consulting with the federal information security incident center.
Continuity of operations plans and procedures	Minimally following	NMB has not established and maintained up-to-date continuity of operations plans and procedures for its information systems. Specifically, its continuity of operations plan has not been updatedsince June 2011 and does not reflect the current information technology environment.
Privacy Practices[c]		
Assign agency official for privacy	Following	NMB has designated its Assistant Chief of Staff as its senior agency official for privacy.
Establish policies and procedures for privacy protections	Minimally following	NMB does not have policies and procedures for privacy protections.

Appendix II: (Continued)

Practice	Extent NMB is following[a]	Example of NMB's status
Privacy impact assessmentsd	Minimally following	NMB has not conducted a privacy impact assessment for itsfinancial management systems, which contain personally identifiable information.
System of records notice[e]	Minimally following	NMB did not issue system of records notice for its financial management systems.

Source: GAO analysis of NMB documents and interviews with NMB officials. | GAO-16-240.

Notes:

[a] We assessed whether NMB is following key practices (NMB is taking appropriate actions and has a formal plan, policy, or other document), partially following (is taking some actions but does not have a formal plan or policy and/or some additional steps must be taken to consider this practice implemented), or minimally following (NMB is taking little or no action to address this particular practice). For more information on our evaluation of NMB's information security and privacy practices in December 2013, see GAO, National Mediation Board: Strengthening Planning and Controls Could Better Facilitate Rail and Air Labor Relations, GAO-14-5 (Washington, D.C.: Dec. 3, 2014).

[b] Key practices from the Federal Information Security Modernization Act of 2014 (FISMA 2014). Information security program and evaluation requirements for federal agencies were established by the Federal Information Security Management Act of 2002 (FISMA 2002). FISMA 2002 was largely superseded by FISMA 2014, which incorporates and continues the requirements of FISMA 2002 applicable to NMB.

[c] Key practices from the Privacy Act of 1974, the E-Government Act of 2002, OMB guidance, and the National Institute of Standards and Technology Special Publication 800-53, Revision 4.

[d] A privacy impact assessment is an analysis of how personal information is collected, stored, shared, and managed in a federal system.

[e] A system of records is a collection of information about individuals under control of an agency from which information is retrieved by the name of an individual or other identifier. System of records notices are posted to agency websites to identify, among other things, the purpose of and individuals covered by information in a system of records, the category of records that are maintained about the individuals, and how the information is shared and routinely used by the agency.

APPENDIX III: COMMENTS FROM THE NATIONAL MEDIATION BOARD

NATIONAL MEDIATION BOARD
WASHINGTON, D.C. 20005
202-692-5000

January 14, 2016

Cindy S. Brown Barnes, Director
Education, Workforce, and Income Security Issues
Government Accountability Office
441 G Street, N.W.
Washington, DC 20548

Dear Ms. Barnes:

This letter is provided in response to the Government Accountability Office draft report *GAO-16-240, National Mediation Board - Progress Made On Some GAO Recommendations to Strengthen Operations, But Key Controls Continue To Be Needed*, dated February, 2016.

The National Mediation Board appreciates the opportunity to provide comments before final publication of the report, and the efforts of GAO to conduct its congressionally mandated review. The Board will review and address the observations made by GAO and the one recommendation for executive action.

As a preliminary matter, it is important to note that many of the functions and matters that GAO makes findings and recommendations regarding involve services contracted out to other federal agencies. The Department of Interior and Bureau of Fiscal Services at the US Treasury Department provide human resources, procurement and financial management services to NMB. Part of the reason NMB uses those services is that those agencies have greater expertise and meet all the security requirements for federal systems. Among other things, this means that NMB has little personally identifiable information in its direct control and does not run its own procurements. It would in fact be a waste of resources for NMB to attempt to evaluate and audit DOI and BFS services when the agencies themselves also do that on a much broader scale.

Additional Actions Needed in Response to GAO's December 2013 Recommendations

Strategic Planning: Develop formal written policies and procedures governing its planning process.

> As noted in the NMB 2014-2019 Strategic Plan, the format and method used to develop the plan was taken directly from guidance found in the Office of Management and Budget, Circular A-ll, July, 2013, which establishes best practices for strategic planning. While the NMB has already been following those policies, the NMB will now use the Circular to formalize its internal policies to mirror those endorsed by OMB.

Performance Goals and Measures: Ensure performance goals meet all guidelines for federal performance management.

> The NMB will consult with OMB and other government labor relations agencies (FMCS, FLRA, and NLRB) regarding possible changes to our measurement and tracking of qualitative goals.

Mechanism to Resolve Audit Findings/Recommendations: Expand the process to address all audits.

> As demonstrated, the NMB has established policies and procedures for responding to financial audit findings. The NMB will also put in place a Standard Operating Procedure (SOP) for responding to audit findings of all other types. It should be noted that the NMB has received a completely unqualified financial audit, all issues related to external and internal audits have been cleared, and all program audit findings have been addressed. There are no outstanding issues related to audits of any kind.

Information Security Program: Develop and implement policies and procedures and assess third-party providers' compliance with security requirements.

> The NMB will develop a SOP for reviewing security audits conducted by all third-party providers. The NMB's third-party providers are large federal agencies with their own mandate to conduct information security audits. The NMB is not positioned, organizationally or with regard to resources, to audit the internal programs of our third-party providers.

Cindy Brown Barnes
January 14, 2016

2

Information Privacy Program: Assess impact on privacy and issue notices about personally identifiable information [PII] NMB uses and shares.

> PII related to NMB employees, contractors, and parties is generally held by the NMB's third-party providers. As with information security, the NMB is not positioned to audit the PII practices of our third-party providers. The NMB can and will develop a SOP for reviewing PII audits conducted by all third-party providers, and the NMB will develop an internal policy for identifying and monitoring employee, contractor, and party PII gathered and held temporarily by the agency.

Rail Grievance and Arbitration Data: Collect data on all cases and analyze them.

> The NMB has instituted a policy that allows for the collection of case data for all cases filed in the arbitration system.

Recommendation for Executive Action: We [GAO] recommend that the Chairman of the National Mediation Board develop and implement policies and processes to reflect the agency's current procurement environment.

> The NMB Chairman and Board Members have directed the NMB Chief of Staff, as the appropriate administrative officer for the Board, to work with the Assistant Chief of Staff for Administration to develop the appropriate procurement policies and processes. As noted above, however, BFS provides procurement services for NMB currently so NMB policies and procedures will be largely subordinate to those of BFS.

General Comments:

> Security continues to be a primary concern for the NMB and particularly for the Information and Communication Technology (ICT) program. During 2015, five security-related training sessions were held for all staff. Two dealt with personal security and were conducted by the Federal Protective Service. One training program was provided online through the Department of Defense. That training addressed information security and personal conduct. The final two training sessions addressed NMB systems specifically and covered basic ICT security on the NMB's cloud system and security issues related to the NMB's online records schedule. Finally, the NMB has begun work with the Bureau of Fiscal Services audit group to do a complete security and risk assessment of the NMB ICT programs.

> Some of GAO's concerns appear to involve a failure to sufficiently document process rather than the agency was non-compliant with any particular requirement. In the area of strategic workforce planning, for example, GAO noted that the internal process for

developing the workforce plan was not documented adequately. The NMB used the standard guidance from OMB and OPM regarding development of the plan and GAO does not appear to disagree. While the NMB appreciates GAOs suggestion and will develop an internal written policy that mirrors the best practices from OMB and OPM's guidance, it is worth noting that the agency had already been following those requirements.

The Board is concerned that the GAO continues to assert that consultation with stakeholders is not adequately done during the agency's planning efforts, even though multiple notations are made in the GAO report to the effect that NMB stakeholders told GAO they had input and were satisfied that their input was heard by the agency. The Board specifically requested input from stakeholders multiple times in multiple venues for its planning initiatives, including posting the draft strategic plan on the NMB web site. It is unclear what additional methods might satisfy GAO's concerns about stakeholder consultation.

If you have any questions or if you require further discussion of any of the comments contained in this response, please have your staff contact the NMB Chief of Staff, Daniel Rainey, at rainey@nmb.gov or 202-692-5015.

Sincerely,

Nicholas Geale, Chairman
The National Mediation Board

Harry Hoglander, Member
The National Mediation Board

Linda Puchala, Member
The National Mediation Board

Cindy Brown Barnes
January 14, 2016

4

End Notes

[1] The RLA was enacted in 1926 to provide a framework for ensuring harmonious railroad labor relations, and amended in 1936 to also cover the airline industry. It establishes several key principles, including the requirement to "exert every reasonable effort" to settle disputes to

avoid interruption to commerce or to the operation of any railroad or airline, and procedures for resolving disputes over pay, rules, or working conditions during collective bargaining, as well as disputes resulting from the interpretation or application of existing collective bargaining agreements. 45 U.S.C. §§ 152, First, Sixth, 153 and 155.

[2] Pub. L. No. 112-95, § 1004, 126 Stat. 11, 147.

[3] GAO, National Mediation Board: Strengthening Planning and Controls Could Better Facilitate Rail and Air Labor Relations, GAO-14-5 (Washington, D.C.: Dec. 3, 2013).

[4] GAO, Standards for Internal Control in the Federal Government, GAO/AIMD-00-21.3.1 (Washington, D.C.: November 1999).

[5] Information security program and evaluation requirements for federal agencies were established by the Federal Information Security Management Act of 2002 (FISMA 2002). FISMA 2002 was largely superseded by the Federal Information Security Modernization Act of 2014 (FISMA 2014) that incorporates and continues the requirements of FISMA 2002 applicable to NMB.

[6] We used key principles for effective strategic workforce planning to assess NMB's October 2014 Workforce and Succession Plan. See GAO, Human Capital: Key Principles for Effective Strategic Workforce Planning, GAO-04-39 (Washington, D.C.: Dec. 11, 2003). We originally developed these criteria as part of a body of work examining issues in strategic human capital management.

[7] To assess NMB's procurement function, we used best practices for acquisition developed in GAO, Framework for Assessing the Acquisition Function at Federal Agencies, GAO-05-218G (Washington, D.C.: September 2005). To develop this framework, we consulted with federal government and industry experts in the areas of human capital, information management, financial management, and acquisition practices and prior GAO work.

[8] For fiscal year 2015, we only looked at contract actions from October 1, 2014, through August 3, 2015, because that was the date the Bureau of the Fiscal Service responded to our data request.

[9] NMB routinely prepared comprehensive, agency-wide financial statements and contracted for independent audits of those financial statements. Allmond and Company, LLC, conducted NMB's fiscal year 2013 through 2015 annual financial statement audits. We reviewed the methodology used to conduct these audits and found them sufficient for our purposes, but did not independently assess the audit findings.

[10] Interviewees for our December 2013 report were identified by issue area experts within GAO and a literature review. See GAO-14-5.

[11] 45 U.S.C. § 154, First. No more than two members of the board can be from the same political party. The board members are required to designate a chairman annually. 45 U.S.C. § 154, Second.

[12] A craft or class consists of those employees who perform the same duties or functions at a given carrier, such as locomotive engineers or pilots.

[13] 45 U.S.C. § 152, Ninth.

[14] 45 U.S.C. § 155, First. In general, mediation is a process through which disputing parties, with assistance from a neutral third party (known as a mediator), seek ways to settle their dispute.

[15] 45 U.S.C. § 153, First (i). Unless otherwise noted, in this report, when we refer to arbitration, we are referring to grievance arbitration.

[16] The arbitration of unresolved grievances in the rail industry takes place before either the National Railroad Adjustment Board, created by the RLA, or adjustment boards established by the parties (rail carriers and unions), known as Public Law Boards or Special Boards of Adjustment. 45 U.S.C. § 153, First (i), Second; 29 C.F.R. § 1207.1. These adjustment boards generally are made up of an equal number of carrier and union representatives. The RLA gave

NMB the authority to create a National Air Transport Adjustment Board (45 U.S.C. § 185), but it has not done so. Instead, in the airline industry, parties jointly create their own temporary special boards of adjustment, called System Boards, through collective bargaining agreements.

[17] OMB, Strategic Plans, Annual Performance Plans, Performance Reviews, and Annual Program Performance Reports, Circular No. A-11, Part 6 (Washington, D.C.: July 2013).

[18] In 1993, Congress passed the Government Performance and Results Act (GPRA), which established strategic planning, performance planning, and performance reporting as a framework for agencies to communicate progress in achieving their missions. Pub. L. No. 103-62, 107 Stat. 285 (1993). The GPRA Modernization Act of 2010 (GPRAMA), enacted in 2011, established some important changes to existing requirements by placing a heightened emphasis on priority-setting, cross-organizational collaboration to achieve shared goals, and the use and analysis of goals and measurements to improve outcomes. GPRAMA enhanced agency-level planning and reporting requirements and required agencies to have additional leadership involvement and accountability. See Pub. L. No. 111-352, 124 Stat. 3866 (2011).

[19] Involving stakeholders is a key practice for strategic planning to (1) help agencies ensure that their efforts and resources are targeted at the highest priorities and (2) help create a basic understanding among the stakeholders of the competing demands that confront most agencies, the limited resources available to them, and how those demands and resources require careful and continuous balancing. Stakeholders for federal agencies include Congress, agency employees, and customers. See GAO, Executive Guide: Effectively Implementing the Government Performance and Results Act, GAO/GGD-96-118 (Washington, D.C.: June 1996).

[20] GAO/AIMD-00-21.3.1.

[21] See 31 U.S.C. § 1115(b). These requirements originated in GPRA and were unchanged by GPRAMA.

[22] Consistent with GPRAMA, OMB defines a performance goal as a statement of the level of performance to be accomplished within a time frame, expressed as a tangible, measurable objective or as a quantitative standard, value, or rate. For implementation of GPRAMA, OMB states that a performance goal includes a performance indicator, a target, and a time period. See OMB, Preparation and Submission of Strategic Plans, Annual Performance Plans, and Annual Performance Reports, Circular No. A-11, Part 6 (July 2014).

[23] We assessed NMB's performance goals, as reported in NMB's fiscal year 2016 performance plan, against OMB guidance implementing GPRAMA requirements. See OMB Circular No. A-11, Part 6 (July 2014). In its fiscal year 2016 performance plan, NMB included performance goals for its administration department as well as each of its program areas (Mediation and Alternative Dispute Resolution, Representation, and Arbitration). NMB did not include measures in its fiscal year 2016 performance plan.

[24] These strategies are (1) selecting a mix of outcome goals of which the agency has varying levels of control, (2) redefining the scope of a strategic goal to focus on a more narrow range of actual activities, (3) disaggregating goals for distinct target populations for which the agency has different expectations, and (4) using data on external factors to statistically adjust for their net effect on the desired outcome. See GAO, Managing for Results: Measuring Program Results that Are Under Limited Federal Control, GAO/GGD-99-16 (Washington, D.C.: Dec. 11, 1998).

[25] Under standards issued by the American Institute of Certified Public Accountants, a control deficiency exists when the design or operation of a control does not allow management or employees to prevent or detect misstatements on a timely basis. A significant deficiency is

one that adversely affects an agency's ability to reliably initiate, authorize, record, process, or report financial data in accordance with generally accepted accounting principles. A material weakness is a significant deficiency, or combination of significant deficiencies, that could result in a material misstatement in financial statements. Because of inherent limitations in internal controls, misstatements, losses, or noncompliance may nevertheless occur and not be detected.

[26] In fiscal years 2010 and 2011, NMB's financial auditor identified a material weakness related to the untimely recording of obligations related to NMB's arbitration services. In 2012, this issue was downgraded to a significant deficiency and remained so until the fiscal year 2015 audit.

[27] Federal internal control standards state that agencies should ensure that the findings of audits and other reviews are promptly resolved. See GAO/AIMD-00-21.3.1.

[28] During NMB's financial statement audit, auditors noted certain matters involving internal control and NMB's operations that warranted management's attention. The auditors issued a management letter to NMB discussing all nonreportable conditions involving NMB's operations.

[29] NMB's financial auditor noted that NMB was unaware of a positive balance in a United States Savings Bond deposit fund, which, as a result, was not reported in NMB's general ledger. Additionally, the auditor noted that because NMB did not have written procedures for performing monthly reconciliations, NMB was unable to determine to whom the funds belonged.

[30] The terms personal information and personally identifiable information are used interchangeably in this report to refer to any information about an individual maintained by an agency, including (1) any information that can be used to distinguish or trace an individual's identity, such as name, Social Security number, date and place of birth, mother's maiden name, or biometric records, and (2) any other information that is linked or linkable to an individual, such as medical, educational, financial, and employment information.

[31] During our initial review, NMB stated its previous in-house data center required changes in response to the president's Cloud First Directive and the Trusted Internet Connection and Data Center Consolidation initiatives.

[32] According to NMB documents, NMB's Enterprise Cloud system supports the agency's mission by providing email, calendars, and records.

[33] The Federal Information Security Modernization Act (FISMA) of 2014 was enacted as Pub. L. No. 113-283, 128 Stat. 3073 and amended chapter 35 of Title 44, U.S. Code. FISMA of 2014 largely supersedes the very similar FISMA 2002, expands the role and responsibilities of the Department of Homeland Security, and retains many of the requirements for federal agencies' information security programs previously set by the 2002 law. See Pub. L. No. 107-347, Title III, 116 Stat. 2899, 2946 (2002).

[34] See 5 U.S.C. § 552a and Pub. L. No. 107-347, § 208, 116 Stat. 2899, 2921.

[35] FedRAMP is a U.S. government program that standardizes how FISMA applies to cloud computing services by providing a consistent approach to security assessment, authorization, and continuous monitoring for cloud products and services.

[36] FISMA 2014, among other things, authorizes DHS to assist OMB with overseeing and monitoring agencies' implementation of security requirements.

[37] We previously reported that small agencies, such as NMB, had not fully implemented requirements of an information security program and face challenges in using information security and privacy guidance and services provided by OMB and DHS. See GAO, Information Security: Additional Oversight Needed to Improve Programs at Small Agencies, GAO-14-344 (Washington, D.C.: June 25, 2014).

[38] GAO/AIMD-00-21.3.1.

[39] Periodic measurement of an agency's progress toward human capital goals and the extent that human capital activities contributed to achieving programmatic goals provides information for effective oversight by identifying performance shortfalls and appropriate corrective actions. See GAO-04-39.

[40] In this review we assessed the extent to which the agency had developed a plan that included the practices identified in our December 2013 report, but we did not independently assess NMB's implementation of the plan. In our December 2013 report, we also noted that OPM evaluated NMB's human capital program in 2007. See GAO-14-5. According to OPM officials, they plan to perform an evaluation of NMB's human capital program in the second half of fiscal year 2016, but have not determined what subjects it will cover.

[41] GAO-04-39.

[42] 45 U.S.C. § 153, First (i). The arbitration of unresolved grievances in the rail industry takes place before either the NRAB or adjustment boards established by the parties (rail carriers and unions), known as Public Law Boards or Special Boards of Adjustment. 45 U.S.C. § 153, First (i), Second; 29 C.F.R. § 1207.1. These adjustment boards are generally made up of an equal number of carrier and union representatives.

[43] Grievance arbitration cases in the rail industry can involve a wide range of grievances, such as wrongful dismissals, unfair labor practices, and rights to additional pay.

[44] NMB offers grievance mediation to parties as an alternate way to resolve grievances that have been filed for arbitration. According to NMB, cases handled through grievance mediation do not contribute to the backlog of arbitration cases and greatly reduce the cost of grievance handling to both the parties and to NMB.

[45] GAO-05-218G.

[46] Contracting officers are authorized to enter into, administer, and/or terminate contracts.

[47] Our work has shown that integrated tracking of contracting and financial data is needed to support management decision making and external reporting requirements. See GAO-05-218G.

[48] According to federal internal control standards, control activities are the policies, procedures, techniques, and mechanisms that enforce management's directives and they should be effective and efficient in accomplishing the agency's control objectives. For example, internal controls and all transactions and other significant events need to be clearly documented and such documentation should appear in management directives, administrative policies, or operating manuals. See GAO/AIMD-00-21.3.1. Our work has shown that policies and processes embody the basic principles that govern the way an agency performs the procurement function. Key principles call for effective policies and processes to govern the planning, award, administration, and oversight of procurement efforts, with a focus on assuring that these efforts achieve intended results. Further, these policies and procedures are to be accompanied by controls and incentives to ensure they are translated into practice. See GAO-05-218G.

[49] GAO-04-39.

End Notes for Appendix I

[1] Pub. L. No. 112-95, § 1004, 126 Stat. 11, 147.

[2] GAO, National Mediation Board: Strengthening Planning and Controls Could Better Facilitate Rail and Air Labor Relations, GAO-14-5 (Washington, D.C.: Dec. 3, 2013).

[3] Interviewees for our December 2013 report were identified by issue area experts within GAO and a literature review. See GAO-14-5.

[4] For fiscal year 2015, we only looked at contract actions from October 1, 2014, through August 3, 2015, because that was the date the Bureau of the Fiscal Service responded to our data request.

[5] NMB routinely prepared comprehensive, agency-wide financial statements and contracted for independent audits of those financial statements. Allmond and Company, LLC, conducted NMB's fiscal year 2013 through fiscal year 2015 annual financial statement audits. We reviewed the methodology used to conduct these audits, but did not independently assess the audit findings.

In: National Mediation Board
Editor: Tina Jimenez

ISBN: 978-1-63485-993-6

Chapter 2

NATIONAL MEDIATION BOARD STRATEGIC PLAN FY 2014 - FY 2019*

National Mediation Board

I. OVERVIEW

The National Mediation Board (NMB) is an independent Executive Branch agency established by the 1934 amendments to the Railway Labor Act (RLA) of 1926. The 1934 amendments to the Act established the NMB's duties and responsibilities as they related to the railroad industry in the United States. In 1936, the Act was expanded to include the airline industry.

The NMB is headed by a three-member Board appointed by the President and confirmed by the Senate. The Board Members annually self-designate a Chairman. The Board Members provide overall leadership and strategic direction for the Board, but have delegated day-to-day oversight and administration to the Chief of Staff and the General Counsel. The Chief of Staff along with the Departmental Directors and General Counsel direct the program operations, which include the Office of Mediation and Alternative Dispute Resolution Services, the Office of Legal Affairs, the Office of Arbitration Services, and the Office of Administration.[1]

---

* This is an edited, reformatted and augmented version of a document released by the National Mediation Board as amended, May 2015.

II. Mission

Based upon the statutory language[2], the National Mediation Board has an overarching mission for the entire agency, and specific supporting missions for each program area within the NMB.

Agency Mission: to promote harmonious labor relations in the airline and railroad industries in the United States in order to best avoid an interruption to commerce or to the operation of any carrier engaged therein.

Representation Mission: to facilitate the orderly determination of representation in the airline and railroad industries in the United States.

Mediation and Alternative Dispute Resolution Mission: to facilitate the settlement of disputes related to pay, work rules, and working conditions, and to develop innovative approaches to dispute resolution and problem solving for carriers and organizations in the airline and railroad industries in the United States.

Arbitration Mission: to facilitate the settlement of disputes arising from the implementation or interpretation of existing agreements covering rates of pay, work rules, and working conditions.

In keeping with the missions outlined in the Act, the NMB's strategic goals will cover the spectrum of labor relations in the airline and railroad industries, from questions concerning whether workers are represented and which group or individual may represent them, to the negotiation of collective bargaining agreements, to resolution of questions regarding performance under established collective bargaining agreements as well as the supporting services that ensure the capacity to realize these goals in an efficient manner.

III. Vision and Values

The NMB will build on its eighty years of success by focusing on its statutory missions and remaining committed to a set of basic organizational values.

Personnel: The NMB is committed to recruiting and maintaining a workforce that is second to none in talent, training, and diversity. We will promote an environment that fosters the continuous development of leadership, technical skills, and professional skills in all employees.

Public Service: The NMB will strive for excellence by providing high quality products and timely services to the parties and the public.

Collaboration: The NMB will foster an open environment where teamwork is utilized and where professional relationships are based on mutual trust, respect, support, cooperation, and communication.

Transparency: The NMB will make appropriate information and data available in order to inform the public, Congress, and stakeholders about its activities.

IV. Organizational Structure

The National Mediation Board consists of six units, and when fully staffed, has fifty-one full time employees as follows.

Board Members (including Confidential Assistants) – six employees.

Office of the Chief of Staff (including Public Information, Information and Communication Technology, and Administrative personnel) – fourteen employees.

Office of Mediation and Alternative Dispute Resolution Services – fifteen employees. Office of Arbitration Services – six employees.

Office of Legal Affairs (including Representation Services) – ten employees.

In addition, the NMB contracts for services in the areas of Information and Communication Technology, Arbitration, Personnel Services, Payroll, Finance, Procurement, and Telephone/Internet Voting.

V. Stakeholder Engagement

The stakeholders in the work done by the National Mediation Board include carrier and organization members in the airline and railroad industries, lawyers and arbitrators who have a practice related to the Railway Labor Act, Congressional oversight committees, and members of the public.

The NMB has developed a number of avenues of communication with stakeholders, all of which are active and all of which channel information, assessments, and recommendations to the NMB.

Dunlop I

The Commission on the Future of Worker-Management Relations[3] (also known as the Dunlop Commission) was the precursor to more focused groups, the Airline Industry Labor-Management Committee[4] and the Joint Labor/Management Rail Freight Committee.[5] These reports, collectively referred to by the NMB as "Dunlop I", made recommendations and set challenges that have guided the NMB for the past two decades.

Dunlop II

In 2009, the NMB formed a successor group to continue the work begun by the Dunlop I Commission. The Dunlop II group[6] consists of representatives from rail and air labor and management, and has been continually active since its creation. The NMB meets with the Dunlop II group at least twice per year to get feedback on agency performance, industry trends, and other information vital to the missions of the NMB.

Section 3 Committee

"Section 3" refers to the section of the RLA that deals with resolution of grievances related to compliance with the terms of collective bargaining agreements in place on airline and railroad properties. The Section 3 Committee consists of principal leaders in the rail industry for both labor and management (e.g., Union Presidents and Vice-Presidents or Directors of Labor Relations for carriers). The NMB meets at least twice yearly with the entire committee to discuss initiatives and get feedback on agency performance in arbitration and grievance mediation.

Arbitration Forum

The Arbitration Forum was formed to obtain feedback from stakeholders who are frequent hands-on users of the Section 3 process. This group includes representatives from rail labor and management as well as a representative from the arbitration community who use the National Railroad Adjustment Board process, the System Board of Adjustment and Public Law Board processes. The Forum meets at least three times each year to review feedback on the Section 3 process and to discuss implementation of NMB policies.

Passenger Rail Conference

Every 18 months, the NMB hosts a Passenger Rail Conference at which representatives from passenger rail labor and management share information about industry trends, critical issues in bargaining, and the status of other agency work in the passenger rail arena.

Freight Rail Symposium

In 2014, the NMB will host the second Freight Rail Symposium, at which representatives of rail labor and management for the freight railroads will have the opportunity to share information about industry trends, critical issues in bargaining, and offer feedback to the NMB regarding the status of agency work with the freight railroads.

Presentations to Stakeholder Conferences

From time to time, carrier organizations and union organizations hold conferences at which the NMB is invited to speak. At these conferences NMB staff and Board Members are able to convey information to the parties and the public and receive feedback about the NMB.

ABA Labor and Employment Law (L&E), Railway-Labor Act Conferences

The American Bar Association L&E meetings feature presentations by NMB staff and Board Members, and enable interaction with members of the bar who practice before the NMB or are involved in collective bargaining with the parties who operate under the RLA.

ABA Section of Dispute Resolution (SDR)

NMB Staff and Board Members regularly offer presentations at the American Bar Association's SDR conference. At the SDR meetings are members of the bar who practice before the NMB, and who are engaged in collective bargaining with parties operating under the RLA. Also in attendance are arbitrators who are members of the NMB roster. NMB staff and Board Members are able to gather feedback on critical issues from attendees at each conference.

Association for Conflict Resolution (ACR)

NMB Staff and Board Members regularly offer presentations at ACR conferences. At the ACR meetings are arbitrators who are members of the NMB roster. NMB staff and Board Members are able to gather feedback on critical issues from attendees at each conference.

National Association of Railroad Referees (NARR)

NMB Staff and Board Members regularly offer presentations and participate in panels at annual NARR conferences. Membership in the NARR is limited to those attorneys and arbitrators engaged in RLA work, the vast majority of whom are members of the NMB arbitrator roster. NMB Staff and Board Members are able to gather feedback on critical issues from attendees at each conference.

National Academy of Arbitrators (NAA)

NMB Staff and Board Members regularly offer presentations and participate in panels at annual NAA conferences. At the NAA meetings are arbitrators who practice in both the airline and railroad industries, many of whom are members of the NMB roster, and some are members of the NARR. NMB Staff and Board Members are able to gather feedback on critical issues from attendees at each conference.

National Bar Association (NBA)

NMB Staff regularly participate in annual conferences of the NBA, attended largely by minority members of the American Bar Association. At the NBA meetings are members of the bar who practice before the NMB and who are engaged in collective bargaining with parties operating under the RLA. Also in attendance are arbitrators who are members of the NMB roster, or who have an interest in joining the NMB roster. NMB staff are able to gather feedback on critical issues from attendees at each conference.

NMB Public Information

The National Mediation Board maintains three public information venues through which feedback from the public is obtained. The NMB web site (www.nmb.gov) is one of the most accessible and informative of government web sites, and is clearly offered as an avenue to contact the agency or to give direct feedback. The NMB Knowledge Store is the default research tool for practitioners who are involved in the NMB's Section 3 process, and for members of the public. A feedback contact is clearly marked on the Knowledge Store and is routinely used to give direct feedback to the agency. Finally, the NMB maintains a public information hot line that allows direct access to agency public information staff, and which is routinely used to give direct feedback to the agency.

VI. Agency-Wide Priority Goals

Priority Goal 1

Training: The NMB will provide quality training and development opportunities for all staff members to ensure that it can continue to provide its services effectively.

Measures:

- No later than one month after the end of each fiscal year, the NMB will have in place for each employee an Individual Development Plan, reviewed and approved by the employee's supervisor.

- The NMB will, annually, review, and revise if necessary, the agency training policy to ensure that all staff have access to remedial, development, and advancement training as appropriate.

Priority Goal 2

Recruitment: The NMB will, consistent with federal government guidelines and regulations, actively recruit high quality, diverse candidates for positions in all agency Offices.

Measure:

- By the end of FY 2014, the NMB will update its recruitment plan, targeting diverse candidates in each of the job categories represented in the NMB work force. The plan will be reviewed and updated periodically to ensure NMB maintains its highly skilled work force.

Priority Goal 3

Retention: The NMB will continue to maintain an accomplished and knowledgeable workforce by creating a positive work environment and opportunities for growth within the agency.

Measures:

- By the end of FY 2014, the NMB will update its succession plan, identifying key skills for each position and, where possible, creating a pathway to advancement within the agency for junior employees. The plan will be reviewed periodically and updated where appropriate.
- The NMB will endeavor to be rated at or above the small agency average in the categories that relate to employee engagement for the annual Office of Personnel Management employee survey in FY 2014. Each year thereafter, the NMB will identify additional specific focuses to improve based on the results of the prior annual employee satisfaction survey.
- By the end of calendar year 2016 and every three (3) years thereafter, the NMB will conduct an internal climate assessment to ascertain areas

where the agency excels and where the agency can improve, and will develop a plan to address any improvements considered necessary.

- By the end of calendar year 2015 and every three (3) years thereafter, the NMB will conduct 360 degree evaluations of all supervisors and managers.

VII. Strategic Goals

NMB Strategic and Program Goals

Administration guidance for performance management and analysis encourages the establishment of strategic goals, program goals, and measures that lend themselves to trend analysis instead of snapshot, report card activity reports.

The NMB has adopted the standard definitions of goals and programs detailed in Circular A-11, Part 6, distributed in August, 2009 and updated in July 2013, by the Office of Management and Budget. In this document, Strategic Goals are overall agency goals that "group multiple program outcome goals." For the NMB, strategic goals are clearly established by statute and relate directly to the statutory mission of the agency.

In Circular A-11, Program Goals are specific to programs and address performance in areas that are of particular scope and independence under the control of programs. Performance Goals in this document will "target levels of performance over time" for each of the programs.

NMB Statutory Strategic Goals

1) The effectuation of freedom of association and employee rights of self-organization where a representation dispute exists.
2) The resolution of disputes arising out of the negotiation of new or revised collective bargaining agreements.
3) The resolution of disputes over the interpretation or application of existing agreements.

VIII. NMB Program Goals

For purposes of this strategic plan, the NMB has adopted the definition of "program" provided by the Office of Management and Budget (OMB): any organized set of activities directed toward a common purpose or goal that an agency undertakes and describe an agency's mission, functions, activities, services, projects, or processes.

Based upon this definition, there are four program areas within the National Mediation Board: Representation, Mediation and Alternative Dispute Resolution, Arbitration, and Administration.

Representation Goals (Office of Legal Affairs - OLA)

Representation Strategic Goal: The effectuation of freedom of association and employee rights of self-organization where a representation dispute exists.

When presented with a question regarding representation, the NMB staff conducts investigations, ascertains the status of the group or individual seeking to represent workers, conducts representation elections, certifies the results of the election, and handles inquiries or challenges to the election.

Representation Program Goals

Goals: Investigate and resolve representation disputes efficiently. Provide effective legal counsel for the agency. Serve as counsel to any Presidential Emergency Boards.

Note: For all Representation Measures, "respond" indicates contact with the party requesting service or information. Supplying all requested information or services may vary in time depending upon the complexity of the request and other factors related to the request.

Objective A: prompt investigation of representation disputes and definitive resolution of employees' representation status for collective bargaining purposes

Measures:

- Respond to representation applications within 2 business days of their receipt by the NMB.

- An NMB investigator will be assigned to investigate representation matters within 2 business days following the initial NMB response, unless the NMB declines to process the application.
- In all cases, the NMB's determination of whether there is sufficient showing of interest to warrant further investigation will be made within 45 calendar days of docketing.
- In all cases, a certification or dismissal will be issued the next business day after the ballot count.
- All non-appellate representation cases will be completed within 90 calendar days of docketing.

Objective B: enhance training and development of OLA staff.
Measures:

- OLA managers will annually engage in career and skill planning with all OLA staff.
- Each staff member will annually update his or her individual development plan (IDP), identifying a course of continuing education that is reevaluated every 12 months. Included in the IDPs are participation in intra-governmental details; continuing legal education courses in the areas of labor and employment law, FOIA, dispute resolution and ethics; management development courses at the Center for Creative Leadership courses at the National Judicial College or Dept. of Justice; and active participation in professional associations.
- General Counsel will create an updated annual departmental training plan to be reviewed and approved by the Chief of Staff and Board.

Objective C: enhance outreach opportunities in the legal, labor relations and alternative dispute resolution communities to better inform stakeholders about developments and increase the skills and experience of OLA employees.
Measures:

- Members of the Office of Legal Affairs will continue to actively participate as presenters and attendees in conferences sponsored by the American Bar Association, American Law Institute, and the Association of Labor Relations Agencies.
- OLA will continue to regularly participate in intra-governmental initiatives with other federal agencies such as the Department of Labor,

National Labor Relations Board, and the Federal Mediation and Conciliation Service.

- OLA attorneys will continue to serve as editors of the Railway Labor Act treatise published by the Bureau of National Affairs to ensure up-to-date information is available to practitioners.
- OLA will foster partnerships with educational institutions to develop and present research, educational programs, and training programs pertaining to labor and employment law and dispute resolution especially in the railway and airline industries.

Objective D: OLA staff will provide prompt and efficient assistance to Presidential Emergency Boards.

Measures:

- Maintain continuous industry and agency communication at a level that provides early preparation for Presidential Emergency Board management.
- All OLA staff will be trained on Emergency Board procedures to ensure that multiple Boards could be staffed if necessary simultaneously and/or if existing staff with experience are unavailable.

Objective E: maintain concise, relevant reference materials that are readily available to the public and which reduce the number of man-hours used to research and respond to inquiries.

Measures:

- OLA will conduct semi-annual reviews of the Representation Manual and web site, updating where appropriate.
- By the end of FY 2014, OLA will review FOIA requests for the last 3 years to determine what, if any, documents requested could be posted on the Knowledge Store to decrease the volume of FOIA requests, and will conduct annual reviews thereafter.
- OLA will expand information available to the public in the representation case e-filing system and Knowledge Store.
- Conduct "customer satisfaction" survey re: OLA materials in the Knowledge Store, Lyceum and website and survey participants regarding what documents and information they would like access to via e-filing or posted in the Knowledge Store.

Objective F: expand the use of technology to further streamline and reduce costs in interference investigations.

Measure:

- Investigate use of voice recognition software and other cost and time saving mechanisms in taking employee statements during interference investigations.

Mediation and Alternative Dispute Resolution Goals (Office of Mediation and ADR Services)

Mediation/ADR Strategic Goal

The resolution of disputes arising out of the negotiation of new or revised collective bargaining agreements.

Under the RLA, organization and carrier representatives must bargain over what are generally known as “major disputes” – i.e., rates of pay, work rules, and working conditions, that ultimately result in collective bargaining agreements. Importantly, in the area of major disputes, the NMB has no authority to impose conditions or to compel the parties to agree to terms other than those to which they mutually and freely agree. The Act clearly establishes the duties of the parties, which includes the foremost duty, the duty of “carriers and employees to settle disputes.”[7] The NMB can offer mediatory assistance, and can to an extent control the pace and form of the negotiations. In the end, however, it is the parties who ultimately maintain control of when and if they reach mutual agreement on collective bargaining terms through mediation under Section 6 of the RLA. Under Section 6, the NMB offers mediation to the parties, and through several non-statutory programs the parties may take advantage of facilitated problem solving and various training programs to improve bargaining skills through the ADR programs.

Mediation Program Goals

Goal 1: to provide prompt and appropriate intervention and assistance for disputes involving pay, work rules, and working conditions (major disputes).

Objective A: provide timely and accurate case processing by updating performance goals and quality control systems for case assignments and case management.

Measures:

- Applications for Mediation or ADR services will be assessed and docketed within two (2) business days of the date on which the request was received.
- Applications that cannot be docketed will be returned to the requesting party with guidance on re-submission within two (2) business days of the date on which the request was received.
- Docketed cases will be assigned a mediator within five (5) business days of the date on which the case was docketed.
- Assigned mediators will make contact with the parties involved in the case within five (5) business days of the date on which the case was assigned.
- Mediators will submit an initial case report, to include a case management strategy, within five (5) business days of the date of the first meeting with the parties.
- Mediators will submit an updated case report within five (5) business days of the date on which any meeting with the parties concludes.

Objective B: provide outstanding case management. *Strategy for Succes.*

The Railway Labor Act (RLA) requires that the parties have "complete independence" in the resolution of disputes arising under the Act. In this statutory environment, NMB mediators may hold meetings, urge the parties to bargain, and engage many strategies to move the parties toward mutual agreement. However, it is the parties who have the responsibility to bargain in good faith and ultimately control the outcome of bargaining. The statutory framework intentionally makes mediation open-ended, and each case is different based on the parties' interests and circumstance, thereby making it difficult to establish hard time frames for case management. Compared to the RLA, for mediators operating under the National Labor Relations Act (NLRA), contracts expire and deadlines drive the behavior of both mediators and parties. Under the RLA, contracts become amendable and the status quo is maintained until the parties reach agreement, or until the Board judges that the parties should be released from mediation. Under the RLA, outstanding case management calls for close monitoring of cases and regular reviews of case strategy. Although statistical analysis of past cases indicates that, on average, cases are concluded within eighteen months and with approximately 50 days of work "at the table," these time frames cannot be used as hard standards as every case is different based on among other things the specific parties and representatives at the table, the external and internal economic circumstances, and other variables.

Measures:

- In each mediator report, due within five (5) days of the end of any meeting with the parties, the mediator will include an updated case management strategy.
- The Senior Mediators, Deputy Chief of Staff, Chief of Staff, and Board Members will conduct quarterly case review meetings to evaluate the status of all cases one (1) year old or older, and to assess and revise the case management plan if appropriate.

Goal 2: provide appropriate and effective mediator training and continuous development.

Objective A: provide training and orientation for new mediators to ensure their ability to successfully mediate major disputes within the rail and air industries.

Measures:

- Within five (5) days of in-processing, each new mediator will receive a briefing book and undergo a standard new employee orientation.
- Within twenty (20) work days, new mediators will have in place an Individual Development Plan based on the standard IDP guidelines for NMB employees.

Objective B: provide state-of-the-art ongoing training for all Mediators. Measures:

- The NMB updated the standard required training for all Mediators in FY 2014 and will review the requirements annually thereafter.
- The NMB will have a mandatory training event encompassing recent developments in the rail or airline industry, or in mediation/ ADR for each of the scheduled Mediator Meetings.

Goal 3: pursue innovation in the delivery of mediation and alternative dispute resolution services.

Objective: to provide Alternative Dispute Resolution programs that offer innovative mediation and problem solving methods to the parties to improve their ability to resolve disputes expeditiously.

Strategy for Success

Mediation and ADR Services will review and update programs and ensure that Mediators are exposed to state of the art ADR approaches to dispute resolution.

Measures:

- By the end of FY 2014, Mediation and ADR Services will have conducted a complete review of all NMB ADR programs to ensure the program reflects best practices and will review the programs periodically thereafter.
- Mediation and ADR staff will attend major dispute resolution conferences (e.g., Association for Conflict Resolution, ABA Section of Dispute Resolution), and at the Mediator Meeting immediately following each major dispute resolution conference, mediators who attended will debrief the entire Mediator corps on information obtained during the conference.

Goal 4: improve efficiency and effectiveness of NMB programs by providing leading online dispute resolution (ODR) technology and techniques to the Mediators and the parties.

Objective A: provide information and expertise in new and evolving technology appropriate for enhancing Mediation/ADR case work.

Measures:

- NMB staff will participate in major professional meetings devoted to online dispute resolution (e.g., CyberWeek and the International ODR Forum), and at the Mediator Meeting immediately following each major ODR conference, mediators who attended will debrief the entire Mediator corps on information obtained during the conference
- At least once yearly during the period covered by this strategic plan, a specific course or program dedicated to ODR will be made available to the Mediator/ADR corps, and to the parties through the NMB Lyceum or in person training.
- Each year, mediators will offer ODR technologyto the parties.

Arbitration Goals. (Office of Arbitration Services)

Arbitration Strategic Goal

to facilitate the settlement of disputes arising from the implementation or interpretation of existing agreements covering rates of pay, work rules, and working conditions.

Once a collective bargaining agreement is in place, disagreements regarding whether the terms of the agreement are being adhered to are referred to as "minor disputes". By statute, the NMB may assign arbitrators to decide minor disputes. In the rail industry, the NMB also pays the arbitrator's fees and costs. A major non-statutory program of the NMB, grievance mediation, offers a consensual method for resolving minor disputes short of arbitration that reduces costs to the parties and the taxpayers and can accelerate resolution.

Arbitration Program Goals

Goal 1: provide outstanding service delivery to internal and external customers.

Measures:

- For requests for service or information from internal customers made before noon, Arbitration staff will be acknowledged on the day the request is made.
- For requests for service or information from internal customers made after noon, Arbitration staff will acknowledged before noon in the following day.
- External requests for assistance or service will be acknowledged within 1 business day of the receipt of the request.
- The Director will make case assignments within two business days of the deadline for submission of requests.
- Cases will be added to the Arbitrator Work Space on the day during which they are received from the Director.
- Valid and proper vouchers for payments to arbitrator contractors will be processed by Arbitration staff within 2 work days of the date of receipt.

- The Director of Arbitration will approve cases for work no later than five (5) work days after the deadline by which arbitrators must request work.

Goal 2: To engage in active roster development for the contract arbitrators serving the airline and railroad industries.

Measures:

- By the end of the second quarter of FY 2015, the NMB will have underway a development program for prospective RLA arbitrators to diversify and expand the pool of contract arbitrators.
- No later than one month after the end of each fiscal year, the Director of Arbitration Services will deliver to the Chief of Staff a report detailing the number and names of arbitrators used during the fiscal year. Where appropriate, the Chief of Staff and Director will use the information to promote greater diversity in the parties' use of arbitrators.

Goal 3: the Office of Arbitration Services will be a center of innovation in the resolution of "minor" disputes.

Measures:

- The Director of Arbitration Services will meet periodically with the Arbitration Forum members to discuss innovations in arbitration and promote the best practices for more efficient management of resources in resolving minor disputes.
- The NMB's Annual Report will include a review of the economic advantages of the NMB's ADR program.

Administration Goals (Office of Administration Services)

Administration Strategic Goal: to support the program missions of the agency and provide outstanding administrative services.

Administration Program Goals

Goal 1: provide outstanding service delivery to internal and external customers.

Measures:

- For requests for assistance or service from internal customers made before noon, Administration staff will respond on the day the request is made.
- For requests for assistance or service from internal customers made after noon, Administration staff will respond before noon in the following day.
- External requests for assistance or service will be responded to within 2 hours of the receipt of the request.
- New Employee Orientation training will be completed for each new employee within one month of the date of employment.
- An updated New Board Member Briefing Book will be available to each new Board Member on the day of her or his confirmation.

Goal 2: provide timely, efficient and responsible stewardship of the NMB's fiscal resources.

Measures:

- The NMB contracting personnel will brief the Office of the Chief of Staff and the Board Members on each new contract awarded and any substantial change or extension of an existing contract to ensure contracts meet the needs of the agency at a reasonable cost.
- By the end of FY 2014 the NMB will establish new written procedures for interfacing with the BFS office responsible for NMB procurement and contracting and update requisition procedures in accord with best practices.

To ensure transparent and accountable payments, no later than one week after the end of each month, the NMB will reconcile arbitrator billing with the office responsible for NMB procurement and contracting at the BFS.

NMB staff will process and pay expense vouchers within 5 work days of receipt of a valid voucher.

Goal 3: ensure agency spending and budgets are transparent and provide the necessary support for each of the agency's missions throughout the whole fiscal year.

Measures:

- On the last day of each month, the Chief Financial Officer will deliver to the Chief of Staff a current budget report.
- On the last day of each quarter of the fiscal year, the CFO will deliver to the COS a review of spending and projection for the remainder of the fiscal year.
- At the end of the fiscal year, the NMB books will be closed and opened for the next fiscal year within three weeks of the last day of the fiscal year.

Goal 4: improve agency efficiency and public communications through cost effective information and communications technology improvements, including implementing Enterprise Architecture (design, secure and document) the emerging cloud, mobile, bring your own device, and other mechanisms

Measures:

- Fully Implement Enterprise Cloud consisting of Google Apps (Mail, Docs), Google Vault, CloudLock by the end of the second quarter of FY 2014.
- Establish a standard user configuration for all agency devices by the end of the second quarter of FY 2014 and update annually where appropriate.
- By the end of FY 2014, create standard data entry methods for all agency technology devices.

Goal 5: continue to ensure that NMB information is secure while maintaining a government leading information and communications technology system.

Measures:

- By the end of FY 2014, the agency will obtain full FedRAMP approval of its system as fully secure and compliant under the Federal Information Security Management Act (FISMA) and has established a number of interim milestones already under way.

- ICT Staff will conduct monthly reviews with the agency Records Officer to ensure that agency records management is fully compliant with National Archives and Records Administration rules.
- Create and have certified a revised security plan for all agency technology by the end of the second quarter of FY 2014.
- The Chief Information Officer will, at the beginning of each fiscal year, and at the beginning of the third quarter of each fiscal year, report to the COS regarding the status of all NMB ICT systems, including plans and schedules for upgrades, security concerns, if any, and other relevant activities.
- The NMB Records Officer will coordinate delivery of NARA and NMB Records Policy training for new hires as part of new employee orientation.
- The NMB Records Officer will coordinate delivery of NARA and NMB Records Policy refresher training for all employees each year.

IX. Major Management Priorities and Challenges

During fiscal year 2013, the Office of Legal Affairs was particularly focused on fine-tuning the NMB implementation of the Federal Aviation Administration Modernization and Reform Act of 2012 (FAA Act), and there remain a few policy issues related to those changes that the NMB will need to address going forward.

Although complex merger and bankruptcy situations involving some of the nation's largest airlines have made work with the airlines particularly challenging recently, the Office of Mediation and ADR Services has continued to manage mediation and alternative dispute resolution cases well within the agency's performance targets.

The level of grievance activity handled through the NMB Arbitration program increased significantly in FY 2013; the parties brought 6,576 cases in FY 2013 compared to only 3,569 cases in FY 2012. This increase is attributed to the recently concluded national round of bargaining among the Class I freight railroads, which has resulted in the filing of grievances concerning the applicability of certain provisions of those agreements. The NMB expects the filings to decline over time. In its ongoing effort to minimize grievance arbitration cases, NMB's Office of Arbitration Services is focusing on increasing the number of arbitrators available to hear and decide cases and also implementing advanced technology to improve the administrative processing of cases.

Despite budget limitations for the last several years, the NMB has been able to continue to provide the same level of exemplary service. Substantial cost savings in contracting, IT and other areas identified by the Chief of Staff have allowed NMB to continue its mission effectively at reduced budget levels. Similarly, partnerships with universities such as Dominican University and Cornell have successfully created shared value for all participants and made valuable and specialized dispute-resolution training available to NMB staff at little or no charge to the taxpayer.

The ability of negotiators to access negotiations/mediation training at a reasonable cost is an ongoing challenge for bargainers and mediators. Corporate and union resources are often stretched and provide no training, or minimal training, in collective bargaining and the mediation process. Third party negotiation training is costly and does not adequately address the RLA statutory mediation process, if at all. This situation negatively impacts the NMB's ability to process mediation cases. The NMB's delivery of basic negotiation and RLA mediation training to the parties in a cost effective manner, either through no cost on-line courses or locality-based classroom training, is a proactive approach to addressing this challenge that the NMB will continue to pursue and improve.

The parties' ability to fashion successful contract ratification campaigns in the era of social media directly impacts NMB mediation resources, and is an ongoing challenge. When a mediated collective bargaining agreement fails the ratification process our staff must return the case to the mediation table and attempt to fashion another Tentative Agreement. On a case-by-case basis the mediator does explore the parties' plan for contract ratification, and in addition to this case-by-case approach to contract ratification the NMB will address this challenge by working with labor and management to establish "Best Practices for Contract Ratification" that includes the social media component. Introduction of these Best Practices to the parties early in the mediation process and integration of this information in our training programs constitute a pro-active global approach to meeting this challenge.

The NMB faces the on-going challenge of efficient delivery of its program services. Nearly all Representation services are provided on-line. The administrative management of arbitration and mediation cases incorporates technology. The actual delivery of Arbitration and Mediation services primarily involves face to face meetings either through arbitration hearings or mediation sessions. On-line hearings and mediation are the rare exception. The cost of face to face interaction continues to escalate as travel costs and travel time increases. Given the advances in technology and the parties' increasing comfort with on-line interactions, the NMB must continually examine the efficient integration of on-line meetings and other "online dispute resolution" avenues in delivery of program services. By continuing to integrate technology-assisted hearings and meetings into arbitration and mediation services on a case-by-case basis, the NMB can begin to track the frequency and effectiveness of this approach. Sharing that documentation with the parties will further legitimize this approach as an alternative to face-to-face hearings and meetings in appropriate situations. This will provide the basis for NMB policies that continue to effectively integrate technology into NMB program services and enhance the efficient use of our resources.

The NMB will continue to make it a priority to provide the best service possible at the budget levels agreed to by Congress and the President, and hopes to use this strategic plan as a baseline to guide its continuous improvement efforts over the course of the next several years.

End Notes

[1] This Strategic Plan has been developed in accordance with guidance found in the Office of Management and Budget, Circular A-ll, July, 2013, found at: http://www.whitehouse.gov/sites/default/files/omb/assets/a11 current year/a11 2013.pdf

[2] The Railway Labor Act, Section 151a, General Purposes. For a full copy of the RLA, see the NMB web site at http://www.nmb.gov/documents/ rla.html. You may have to copy this hyperlink directly into your Internet Browser.

[3] The Commission was formed to look at worker-management relations across all sectors. The Commission published its report in December, 1994.

[4] The Air Committee issued its report in April, 1996.

[5] The Rail Committee issued its report in August, 1996.

[6] The first Dunlop II report was issued in 2010.

[7] The Railway Labor Act, Section 152, First, Duty of Carriers and Employees to Settle Disputes. For a full copy of the RLA, see the NMB web site at http://www.nmb.gov/documents/rla/html.

In: National Mediation Board
Editor: Tina Jimenez
ISBN: 978-1-63485-993-6

Chapter 3

FREQUENTLY ASKED QUESTIONS: MEDIATION*

National Mediation Board

GENERAL INFORMATION

The Railway Labor Act (RLA) requires labor and management to make every reasonable effort to make and maintain collective bargaining agreements within the airline and railroad industries, without disruption of airline or railroad transportation services. Mediation of collective bargaining agreements in these industries are the only disputes within the National Mediation Board's (NMB) jurisdiction.

Negotiation disputes in the non-rail and non-airline private sector are handled by the Federal Mediation and Conciliation Service (www.fmcs.gov) under the Labor Management Relations Act. Collective bargaining representation of employees in the Federal sector (United States government employees) is administered by the Federal Labor Relations Authority pursuant to the Civil Service Reform Act of 1978, Title VII. (www.flra.gov) Collective bargaining representation of other public sector employees (state, county and municipal government employees) varies and depends on whether there is a state or local law which permits collective bargaining.

---

* This is an edited, reformatted and augmented version of information from the following web site (viewed June 2016): http://www.nmb.gov/services/mediation/frequently-asked-questions-mediation/

One of the purposes of the RLA is to provide for the prompt and orderly settlement of collective bargaining disputes. As provided for in the RLA, the National Mediation Board (NMB) is responsible for providing mediation services to help the parties reach a settlement should the parties fail to reach an agreement during direct negotiations. If the parties are unable to reach a voluntary agreement to establish or modify a collective bargaining agreement, either party may apply for the mediation services of the NMB. Once mediation is invoked, the NMB conducts mediation meetings until an agreement is reached or until the NMB concludes no agreement can be reached despite its best mediatory efforts. If the NMB reaches this conclusion, it urges both sides to resolve their dispute through binding arbitration. Upon rejection of the proffer of arbitration by either party, the NMB releases the parties into a 30 day cooling off period. During the cooling off period, neither side can alter the status quo. At the end of 30 days, the parties either reach an agreement or engage in self help. In some situations, the parties may be required to participate in a Presidential Emergency Board (PEB) and defer any self help action until 30 days after the PEB makes its recommendation.

These questions and answers are meant to provide general guidance only. They do not provide definitive determination of any mediation matter and are not to be construed as legal opinions that may be cited in any administrative, legal, or arbitral proceeding.

1. Q: When do collective bargaining agreements expire under the RLA?

A: Under the RLA, collective bargaining agreements do not expire; instead they become subject to change as of a specified date and upon "notices of intent" by the parties to change some or all of the elements of the agreement. Until a mutually newly negotiated agreement is accepted by both parties, the provisions of the original agreement remain in full force. This is commonly referred to as "status quo."

2. Q: How do parties initiate negotiations under the RLA

A: The parties exchange notices of intent to change or amend the existing contract. These formal notices are referred to as "Section 6″ notices.

3. Q: What are "direct negotiations"?

A: Direct negotiation is the first step in contract negotiations under the RLA, during which the parties meet without the assistance of a mediator.

4. Q: How long does it normally take to negotiate agreements under the RLA?

A: The length of negotiation, including both direct and mediation varies with each case. Normally, the complexity and number of issues bargained-over are the key determinants.

5. Q: Does the NMB use methods other than traditional mediation to assist parties in reaching agreements?

A: Yes. The NMB has initiated a program to train parties in the principles of Facilitated Problem Solving. This training program is voluntary, and is offered upon the request of the parties. Facilitated Problem Solving is a negotiations method which focuses on the interests of the parties and finding mutually acceptable solutions to issues. Facilitated Problem Solving Training is a 1.5 day training program designed to illustrate problem solving approaches through interactive exercises. Should the parties decide to introduce this approach in their negotiations, the NMB will provide a Facilitator to assist the parties in implementing the process.

6. Q: If a case is in litigation, does that mean the RLA isn't working?

A: No. Under the RLA, the NMB does not have jurisdiction over circumstances such as a party's failure to bargain in good faith or failure to adhere to the status quo provisions of the RLA. Therefore, if either party feels that the other is violating the RLA, it is appropriate to seek a remedy in court.

APPLICATION FOR MEDIATION

7. Q: What happens if the parties cannot reach an agreement in direct negotiations?

A: If either party believes an agreement cannot be reached in direct negotiations, that party can apply for mediation with the NMB. Upon application, the NMB will docket the application and assign a mediator to the case.

8. Q: Can the parties file a joint mediation application?

A: Yes, parties may file jointly with the NMB for mediation services.

9. Q: Do both parties have to sign the application for mediation?

A: No, only the party applying for mediation services must sign the application. The signature must be from the highest authority in the organization, i.e., an officer of either the Union or the Company. If the parties file jointly, then both parties must sign the application.

10. Q: Where do we get the mediation application?

A: Applications for mediation may be obtained through the NMB web site or from the Deputy of Chief of Staff office at the NMB.

11. Q: What happens after the application is received by the NMB?

A: The application is first reviewed to ensure that it is completed properly and appropriately, and if so, the case is then docketed.

MEDIATION PROCESS

12. Q: How are mediators assigned to cases?

A: When an application for mediation is received, the Director of Mediation and Senior Mediators consult concerning case assignment. They consider a variety of factors, including individual work loads, mediator availability, schedules, desires of the parties, the history of a given mediator with the parties, mediator background, complexity of the case, and other factors.

13. Q: What kind of background or experience do the NMB mediators have?

A: NMB mediators typically come from either Union or Company backgrounds and have extensive labor relations experience in either the rail or airline industries. Mediator biographies may be found on the NMB web site.

14. Q: During the mediation process, what is the role of the mediator?

A: The role of the mediator is to assist the parties with productive dialog on their issues. The mediator can and will use a variety of techniques to ensure this does occur.

15. Q: Can the NMB determine where the parties will meet when they are in mediation?

A: The courts have held that the NMB has the authority to establish where and when the parties will meet while in mediation. Normally, however, the meeting site and dates are mutually agreed upon among the parties and the mediator.

16. Q: Can the NMB determine when and/or how often the parties will meet when they are in mediation?

A: Again, meetings are normally established by mutual agreement among the parties and the mediator, but during mediation the NMB does have the authority to dictate when the parties will meet, for how long they will meet, and when meetings will be recessed.

17. Q: How long does mediation last?

A: There is no time limit for the mediation process. It can take just a few meetings, or it can take many months, depending upon the complexity of the negotiations and many other factors unique to each contract negotiation. The NMB has the authority to decide when and if to end mediation. Under the RLA, the NMB ceases mediation efforts when it concludes that all reasonable efforts to reach a voluntary agreement through mediation have failed.

18. Q: What does "status quo" mean?

A: "Status quo" is used to describe the terms of the contract in place at the beginning of direct negotiations. During direct negotiations, mediated negotiations, and any cooling off periods after mediated negotiations, neither party may violate the status quo by making unilateral changes in wages, benefits, or working conditions.

19. Q: Why does the NMB Recess a case during mediation?

A: Recess is one of the many tools a mediator uses in managing a Mediation case. If a case is recessed by a mediator, it is for a specific purpose related to the particular facts of the given case.

PROFFER OF ARBITRATION

20. Q: What is a "proffer of arbitration"?

A: When the NMB believes that further mediation efforts will not result in an agreement, it issues a proffer of arbitration, which is an offer to the parties to arbitrate any remaining issues.

21. Q: Why doesn't the NMB make a proffer of arbitration when one of the parties asks for it?

A: Under the RLA, the NMB is responsible for making its best efforts to help the parties reach an agreement without resorting to self-help. While it will listen to requests from the parties for a release, it is the NMB's responsibility to keep parties in mediation until it has expended all reasonable efforts to reach an agreement.

22. Q: What happens if either party rejects the proffer of arbitration?

A: If either party rejects the proffer of arbitration, the NMB releases the parties from mediation and they enter a 30-day count down, or cooling off, period.

COOLING OFF PERIODS

23. Q: What happens during the cooling off period?

A: Normally the NMB invites the parties to meet during the cooling off period in order to further mediate an agreement. These meetings are often referred to as "public interest mediation" or "super mediation."

24. Q: What if no agreement is reached during the 30-day cooling off period?

A: If no agreement is reached by the end of the 30-day cooling off period, the parties are free to exercise "self-help." This means that the Union is free to strike or engage in other activity, and the Carrier is free to impose its last best offer or temporarily cease operations or engage in other self-help activity, unless a PEB is created.

PUBLIC INTEREST MEETINGS

25. Q: What are public interest meetings?

A: During the 30 day cooling off period the NMB will call the parties back to the table for further discussions. These meetings are referred to as public interest meetings or super mediation meetings. Generally, these meetings are called at or near the end of the count down period, but they can be called at any time during the 30 day time frame.

PRESIDENTIAL EMERGENCY BOARD (PEB)

26. Q: What is a "Presidential Emergency Board' (PEB)?

A: During the 30-day cooling off period, the NMB makes a determination regarding the impact of a strike. Pursuant to Section 160 of the RLA, the NMB "notifies" the President that in its "judgement" the dispute between a carrier and its employees cannot be adjusted and "threaten[s] substantially to interrupt interstate commerce to a degree such as to deprive any section of the country of essential transportation service." Once the President receives such notification, the President may, "in his discretion, create a board to investigate and report on such dispute. The NMB submits a recommended list of potential neutrals to the President. The PEB usually has 30 days to develop a proposed agreement and present that agreement to the parties for consideration. After the PEB delivers its proposed agreement, there is a further 30-day cooling off period.

27. Q: What happens if either party rejects the PEB's proposed agreement?

A: If either party rejects the PEB's proposal, the parties may, after the 30-day cooling off period, engage in self-help.

28. Q: Is there any circumstance in which the parties are constrained from engaging in self-help after rejecting a PEB's proposal?

A: Yes. It is possible for the Congress to intervene and legislatively mandate a settlement.

In: National Mediation Board
Editor: Tina Jimenez
ISBN: 978-1-63485-993-6

Chapter 4

FREQUENTLY ASKED QUESTIONS: ARBITRATION*

National Mediation Board

1) Q: What is the daily pay rate for arbitrators on the NMB Roster of Arbitrators?

A: Arbitrators are paid on a per case basis.

2) Q: Is there a separate roster for airline arbitrators?

A: No. The NMB has a single Roster of Arbitrators from which arbitrators can be selected for both airline and railroad cases.

3) Q: What is a Special Board of Adjustment (SBA)?

A: A Special Board of Adjustment is a tribunal set up by agreement on an individual railroad and with a single labor organization to decide specifically) designated grievances. Such disputes could be sent to the appropriate division of the NRAB for adjudication, but the parties, by voluntary agreement, submit the grievances to this type of board.

---

* This is an edited, reformatted and augmented version of information from the following web site (viewed June 2016): http://www.nmb.gov/about-nmb/officials-staff/nmb-board/office-of-arbitration-services/frequently-asked-questions-arbitration/.

4) Q: What is a Public Law Board (PLB)?

A: A Public Law Board is a tribunal established pursuant to Public Law 89-456 which authorized the establishment of special boards of adjustment on individual railroads. Unlike the SBA, which must be established upon agreement of both parties, the PLB can be established upon the written request of either party.

5) Q: What is the National Railroad Adjustment Board (NRAB)?

A: Set up by the Railway Labor Act under the 1934 amendments, this entity is composed of equal numbers of representatives from labor and management. It is their responsibility to hear and decide grievances which have been appealed to the Railroad Adjustment Board from the various carrier properties. Its decisions are final and binding on both parties to the dispute, subject to extraordinarily narrow court review. The NRAB has its own rules known as Circular #1. The NRAB is headquartered in Chicago, IL.

6) Q: What is the relationship between the NRAB and the NMB?

A: The NMB provides staff support for the NRAB. The NMB by law has authority over the expenditure of funds for the activities of the NRAB.

7) Q: Who can file a claim?

A: Any individual employee of a carrier, union official or carrier official can file a claim at the NRAB.

8) Q: How do I file a claim?

A: Please contact the NRAB for instructions on how to file a claim.

9) Q: Where do I file my claim?

A: File your claim with the NRAB via US Postal Service, email or fax.

The address is: National Railroad Adjustment Board of the National Mediation Board 844 North Rush Street. Room 944 Chicago. IL 60611-2092

Ph: 312-751-4688, Fax: 312-751-4681, Email: NRAB@NMB.GOV

10) Q: Does the NMB handle appeals?

A: No. The NMB has no authority to handle appeals of arbitration awards. Under the statute, awards can only be modified in Federal Court. Individuals or organizations must file suit in Federal Court. The NMB has no authority to hear appeals in either industry.

11) Q: I need legal assistance - can the NMB assist me?

A: No. The NMB cannot give legal advice. If you need legal advice, you must retain your own attorney. Check your local bar association for listings. The NMB cannot provide any referrals or advice.

12) Q: How are Arbitrators selected to handle cases?

A: The arbitrator is chosen by the parties. When the parties are unable to agree on an arbitrator, the parties may request that the NMB provide a list of Arbitrator names. In that instance, the NMB Office of Arbitration Services generates a list, generally referred to by the parties as a Strike List, through a random numeric selection process from the NMB Roster of Arbitrators. The parties select an arbitrator from the strike list. Requests for Strike Lists are infrequent.

13) Q: How can an arbitrator find out if he/she was included on a strike list?

A: The arbitrator can find out is he/she was included on a strike list by contacting the Office of Arbitration Services at arb@nmb.gov.

In: National Mediation Board
Editor: Tina Jimenez

ISBN: 978-1-63485-993-6

Chapter 5

FREQUENTLY ASKED QUESTIONS: ADR SERVICES*

National Mediation Board

1. Q: What is Alternative Dispute Resolution (ADR)?

A: ADR is an approach to disputes that allows parties to discuss and develop their interests in order to resolve the underlying issues and problems in their bargaining or grievance handling processes. This is done through facilitated problem solving process. The discussion is facilitated by an impartial third party who is there to help the parties develop a productive dialogue.

2. Q: What is Facilitated Problem Solving?

A: Facilitated Problem Solving is a process by which the parties outline the problems to be solved, clearly define the issues, and discuss the interests associated with the issues. Using a "brainstorming" process, the parties develop options which are potential solutions.

* This is an edited, reformatted and augmented version of information from the following web site (viewed June 2016): http://www.nmb.gov/services/adr/adr-services-frequently-asked-questions/.

3. Q: What are the benefits of using ADR in Labor-Management relationships?

A: ADR allows everyone to have an active part in the decision-making process. Solutions are adopted by consensus, and reflect an understanding of the interests of all parties. As a result, the solutions are tailored to the needs of the participants.

ADR encourages creative, innovative solutions, moving away from the traditional win/lose results of adversarial proceedings. ADR focuses the parties on the substance of issues, not whose turn it is to make the next proposal.

ADR resolves disputes while preserving relationships, and thereby helps create a productive working environment.

4. Q: What types of ADR services does the NMB offer?

A: The NMB offers ADR services that target contract bargaining, grievance mediation, and problem solving outside the normal contract and grievance environments. The NMB provides training to the parties and then offers facilitation to the parties to help them get started in their process. Both the training and the facilitation are free to the parties.

The NMB also conducts presentations at large union and management meetings and conferences to promote the use of Facilitated Problem Solving and Grievance Mediation and other improved problem-solving techniques.

5. Q: Is the NMB's ADR program voluntary?

A: Yes. In order for ADR services to be effective, both parties must support the effort.

6. Q: How much lead time should the parties give the NMB when they desire training?

A: If you wish to schedule face-to-face training, your request for training should be as far in advance as possible to ensure that the dates you want will be available. The NMB recommends that you call about six months in advance of your estimated *first bargaining session* for contract negotiations. Training should be done early because during the training you will learn new ways of preparing for bargaining.

7. Q: Who does the training and facilitation at the NMB?

A: The training and facilitation are done by ADRS staff and by NMB Mediators who deliver both traditional mediation service and ADR services. It is the NMB's desire to have the training done by experienced staff who actually do the facilitation, so they can continuously update the training with new ideas learned from the actual facilitation of Contract or Grievance Mediation cases.

8. Q: Who should attend the training?

A: All participants from both sides who will be involved in the bargaining or grievance handling process.

9. Q: Where is the training held?

A: Face-to-face training is held at the NMB offices; however, arrangements may be made to accommodate the parties under special circumstances at a mutually agreeable location other than the NMB. Online training can be taken from any Internet capable computer.

10. Q: Is there a fee for the training?

A: No. Similar training services would cost several thousand dollars. The NMB absorbs the cost but asks the parties to attend the training in Washington.

11. Q: How do I get more information or ask for assistance or training?

A: For more information about the NMB's ADR program visit http://www.nmb.gov/about-nmb/officials-staff/adr-contacts/ . Copies of the ADR brochure, training dates, and a Training Request form are also located on this web site.

12. Q: What is ODR?

A: ODR (Online Dispute Resolution) is, generally, the use of technology to assist in dispute resolution. For example, parties can use web-based conferencing to prepare for bargaining sessions, to hold bargaining sessions, or to prepare contract language without having to meet face to face. Parties can use online brainstorming to discuss ideas and prepare for the development of solutions to mutually identified problems. ODR technology can also be used in face to face sessions to manage information and make the sessions more efficient. The NMB also offers an online workspace that can be configured to offer secure document sharing and joint editing of documents. One set of parties told the NMB that using technology in the sessions probably saved them "one day a week" in terms of the time it took to address all the issues.

In: National Mediation Board
Editor: Tina Jimenez
ISBN: 978-1-63485-993-6

Chapter 6

FREQUENTLY ASKED QUESTIONS: REPRESENTATION*

National Mediation Board

GENERAL INFORMATION

One of the purposes of the Railway Labor Act (RLA) is to effectuate employees' rights to self- organization. The RLA provides that employees shall have the right to organize and bargain collectively through representatives of their own choosing. It is the National Mediation Board's (NMB or Board) duty to resolve any disputes among employees as to who are their collective bargaining representatives. The NMB investigates these disputes, ensuring peaceful resolutions without disruption to interstate commerce.

The NMB investigates representation disputes in the railroad, commuter railroad, and airline industries only. Collective bargaining representation of employees in other private industries is administered by the National Labor Relations Board pursuant to the National Labor Relations Act. (www.nlrb.gov.) Collective bargaining representation of employees in the Federal sector (United States government employees) is administered by the Federal Labor Relations Authority pursuant to the Civil Service Reform Act of 1978, Title VII. (www.flra.gov.) Collective bargaining representation of other public sector

* This is an edited, reformatted and augmented version of information from the following web site (viewed June 2016): http://www.nmb.gov/services/representation/frequently-asked-questions-representation/.

employees (state, county and municipal government employees) varies and depends on whether there is a state or local law which permits collective bargaining.

These questions and answers are meant to provide general guidance only. They do not provide definitive determination of any representation matter and are not to be construed as legal opinions that may be cited in any administrative, legal or arbitral proceeding.

BASICS

1. Q: What is the role of the NMB in representation matters?

A: It is the NMB's duty to investigate and resolve representation disputes in the railway and airline industries.

2. Q: How do representation disputes come to the NMB?

A: A labor organization (organization) or an individual employee can request that the NMB investigate an alleged representation dispute by filing Form NMB-1,"Application for Investigation of Representation Dispute," available at: Investigation of Representation Dispute Form – NMB 1 (https://storage.googleapis.com/dakota-dev-content/Form-NMB-1-Investigation-of-Representation8-15-14.doc). The organization or individual is also required to file a "Notice of Appearance" with the application which is available at the same link.

3. Q: Who investigates representation matters?

A: Representation investigations are conducted and supervised by the NMB's Office of Legal Affairs.

4. Q: What are the procedures for investigating representation applications?

A: The procedures are detailed in the NMB Representation Manual (Manual) available at: Representation Manual (https://storage.googleapis.com/dakota-dev-content/october-2015-final-manual.pdf). Generally, an organization or individual seeking representation rights must file an application requesting an investigation. The application must be supported by authorization cards. In appropriate cases, an NMB investigator determines: the appropriate craft or class; the eligible voters; whether an election will occur, and; the schedules for a Telephone Electronic Voting (TEV) and Internet Voting election.

APPLICATIONS

5. Q: What is an authorization card?

A: An authorization card is a card or document signed by the employee which states that the employee desires to be represented by an organization or individual for collective bargaining purposes. Authorization cards must have the name of the organization or individual seeking to represent the craft or class, and must be signed and dated by the employee. Typically, authorization cards also include the following information: employee address, telephone number, job title, employee number, and social security number. The NMB compares the signed authorization cards to the List of Potential Eligible Voters supplied by the carrier to determine the percentage of employees signing authorization cards (generally referred to as the "showing of interest"). The employee signature on every authorization card is checked against the signature sample provided by the carrier, and the NMB also checks that the date is valid.

The language on authorization cards must be unambiguous and the NMB must be able to determine the employee's intent. In an accretion application, the authorization cards must be unambiguous and state clearly the sole purpose of the card. The NMB will not accept authorization cards requesting a representation election as support for accretion applications or certification by card check. Cards which both request an election and authorize the applicant to represent the employees will also not be accepted as support for accretion applications or certification by card check.

6. Q: What is the mandatory format for the Carrier's List of Potential Eligible Voters?

A: The Carrier must deliver to the Board's Office of Legal Affairs by 10 a.m., ET, on the date specified in the docketing letter, three copies of an alphabetized list of potential eligible voters and a copy of the alphabetized list on a diskette or CD as a Microsoft Excel file. The format for the List of Potential Eligible voters provided below must be followed.

Specifically, the format of the List of Potential Eligible Voters must be prepared in five columns or fields exactly as shown in the sample format in the docketing letter (columns A, B, C, D, E, only). There must not be any other information or data in the file, diskette, or CD, except as displayed in the five columns or fields on the sample format. The data in the Microsoft Excel file is contained in cells. The column headers, also known as field headers, must appear in the first row of cells only. Therefore, the first row is for column headings only, and all subsequent lines contain only voter information. The Carrier must not include any hidden columns or fields in the Microsoft Excel file. Also note that the employee middle initial appears with the first name. There is no separate column or field for the middle initial. In addition, no other data should appear above the column headings.

The mandatory Microsoft Excel format can be downloaded at (http://www.nmb.gov/documents/carriers_template.xls). Carrier representatives should contact the NMB Elections Administrator at 202-692-5040, if they have any questions about the correct format for the list of potential eligible voters.

7. Q: What is a showing of interest?

A: A showing of interest is the percentage of the craft or class that has signed authorization cards. An application must be supported by a 50% showing of interest, in the form of employee authorization cards. Authorizations will be considered invalid if dated more than one year prior to the date on the NMB application.

8. Q: Can an employee in the craft or class sign an authorization card for more than one organization?

A: Yes.

9. Q: What is an Intervenor?

A: Once an organization has filed an application, another organization may intervene in the representation dispute and place itself on the ballot by presenting authorization cards signed by at least 50% of the employees in the craft or class.

10. Q: How can employees change their labor organization?

A: Employees can change their labor organization by signing authorization cards for another organization, which then files an application and "wins" an election.

11. Q: How can employees decertify their current representative without getting another one?

A: A majority of valid votes must be cast for no representation.

12. Q: Can employees form and elect their own union?

A: Yes, employees can form their own organization if they submit an application supported by a sufficient showing of interest.

INVESTIGATION

13. Q: What does the NMB do after an application is received?

A: The general procedure is for the NMB to docket the application, assign it an R-case number, and designate an Investigator who will handle the case investigation. The docketing letter sets forth a time schedule for the carrier to provide a list of potential eligible voters and signature samples. If the NMB notes anything unusual about the application (for example, an unusual craft or class, a jurisdictional question, or an accretion), the NMB does not docket the application, but gives the matter a CR-file number and conducts a pre-docketing investigation.

14. Q: What is a craft or class?

A: Craft or class is a term used for the group of employees the applicant seeks to represent. Crafts or classes must be system-wide.

15. Q: What factors are considered in determining the proper craft or class?

A: The Board considers several facts in determining a proper craft of class including: the composition and relative permanency of the employee grouping along craft or class lines; the functions, duties and responsibilities of the employees; the general nature of the work performed, and; the community of interest between job classifications. See Manual Section 9.1 at: Representation Manual (https://storage.googleapis.com/dakota-dev-content/october-2015-final-manual.pdf).

16. Q: Who is eligible to vote in the election?

A: All employees working in the craft or class and who are employed as of the last day of the last payroll period prior to the receipt of the application by the NMB are eligible to vote in the election. Employees severing their employment relationship (e.g., by resignation, termination, retirement, death, or promotion) during the balloting period are normally removed from the list. See Manual Section 9.2 at: Representation Manual (https://storage.googleapis.com/dakota-dev-content/october-2015-final-manual.pdf).

17. Q: Who is ineligible to vote in the election?

A: Employees who do not have an employer-employee relationship, for example management officials, contractor employees, or discharged employees. See Manual, Section 9.2 at: Representation Manual (https://storage.googleapis.com/dakota-dev-content/october-2015-final-manual.pdf).

18. Q: Does the NMB provide home addresses to organizations in representation campaigns?

A: The NMB does not provide home addresses to organizations in representation elections. In extraordinary circumstances, where the NMB determines that due to prior interference with the laboratory conditions by the carrier or voter confusion, the NMB may provide the home addresses of eligible voters to the organization.

19. Q: Can a union be certified by the NMB without an election?

A: Yes. If there is only one labor organization applying for representation, and the organization and the carrier agree in writing to a certification based on a check of authorization cards, the NMB can authorize the check of authorizations instead of an election. If a majority of the craft or class has signed authorizations, the organization will be certified without an election.

20. Q: Can my job or position be added or accreted to an existing certified craft or class without an election?

A: Yes. An organization which is certified to represent the craft or class may file an application supported by a showing of authorization cards seeking to accrete jobs or positions into the craft or class. The Investigator then determines if the position(s)' duties and responsibilities share a sufficient community of interest with the craft or class. If the position(s) share a community of interest, and if the number of employees accreted are fewer than those in the total craft or class, the NMB will accrete the employees in that position in the craft or class without an election.

VOTING

21. Q: How are NMB representation elections conducted?

A: Most elections are conducted by Telephone Electronic Voting (TEV) and Internet Voting. Approximately three weeks prior to the tally, each voter is mailed Voting Instructions explaining how to vote. In a standard TEV and Internet Voting election, employees either call in to cast their vote or access the Board's voting website. The way to vote for representation is to select one of the "Yes" options. The way to vote for no representation is to select the "No" option for no representative. The votes are tallied electronically. The results of the tally are provided to the organization(s) and the carrier in writing.

22. Q: Is Telephone and Internet Voting confidential?

A: Yes. All NMB voting is by secret ballot. To access the TEV and Internet Voting system, the voter must enter a confidential, randomly-assigned, twelve-digit Access Code. An Access Code is assigned to a single voter in a single representation election conducted by the Board, and is never used again. A voter's name and Access Code are known only to the voter and to the Election Administrator at the NMB. The confidential Access Code is mailed directly to the employees' homes. Requests for duplicate Access Codes must be made in writing and signed by the individual employee. Use of another voter's Access Code is prohibited by 18 U.S.C. § 1001. The NMB does not disclose the ballot choice of any voter.

23. Q: How is the winner of an election determined?

A: If an organization or individual receives a majority of the valid votes cast, it will be certified as the representative. If the majority of votes cast are for no representation, no representative will be certified.

24. Q: Is the NMB eliminating mail ballots?

A: No. In general, the NMB will be conducting elections using TEV and Internet Voting. The Board may use other appropriate methods, including mail ballots, as it is permitted under Section 2, Ninth.

25. Q: When was TEV implemented?

A: TEV was implemented on September 30, 2002, and Internet Voting was implemented on October 1, 2007.

26. Q: What if there is a computer failure?

A: The election system operated by the NMB's contractor has several backup power and computer systems. If one system fails, another system would pick up. This seamless process ensures that any system failure will not affect a voter's ability to vote. Further, the NMB's elections run for a period of three weeks minimum, allowing participants many opportunities to access the Internet or to use the telephone.

27. Q: How does the system prevent groups of voters from getting together for voting parties?

A: The system maintains multiple, detailed, independent audit trails which allow the contractor to substantiate election results and address election challenges. Therefore, the TEV and Internet voting system improves the Board's ability to investigate allegations of voting parties.

28. Q: How do voters vote no?

A: If a voter wishes to vote against representation, they select the phone prompt or internet phrase: "No. I vote for no representative."

29. Q: Can voters still "write-in" candidates?

A: Yes. They can "speak-in" at the prompt to vote for "any other organization or individual," on the TEV system or "write-in" their selection on the NMB's Internet Voting website. A voter must affirmatively"speak-in" (telephone) or "write-in" (Internet) the name of an individual or organization to cast a valid vote. Recording silence or the phrase "Any Other Organization or Individual" as a "write-in" or "speak-in" vote is no longer a valid vote. See Manual Sections13.304-1 and 13.304-2.

30. Q: What prevents voters from voting multiple times?

A: The TEV/Internet Voting system locks out a user after repeated incorrect Access Code entries. This lockout also prevents hackers from "programmatically" discovering user Access Code combinations. In addition, as the phone and Internet systems are linked, voters are prevented from voting more than once regardless of which medium they choose to vote with.

31. Q: How are eligibility rulings and status changes handled under the TEV and Internet Voting system?

A: The same as under the mail ballot system. Electronic removal and addition of voters would be substituted for the current manual process.

32. Q: What records regarding the TEV and Internet Voting system will the parties have access to?

A: The participants will have access to information available to them under the Freedom of Information Act and the Privacy Act.

33. Q: What is the process for requesting duplicate Telephone and Internet Voting instructions?

A: The process for requesting duplicate Telephone and Internet Voting instructions will be set forth in instructions sent to each voter as well as posted at each base. The voter must request duplicate Telephone and Internet Voting instructions in writing and no group requests will be honored.

34. Q: Can voters change their votes?

A: Yes and no. While a voter is in the TEV or Internet Voting system, he/she will be prompted to confirm his/her choices and can make changes accordingly. Once the ballot is successfully cast, the voter cannot re-access the TEV or Internet Voting system and "change" the vote. The system will recognize this as an attempt to vote more than once.

35. Q: What do voters do if they are experiencing problems voting?

A: If a voter experiences problems, he/she should try again. If that fails, the voter should contact the NMB at the number provided on the Notice of Election/Telephone and Internet Voting Instructions and an OLA staff member will assist them.

36. Q: Do voters need any special equipment to participate in TEV and Internet Voting Elections?

A: Voters need access to a touch tone phone or access to the Internet in order to vote. Voters will not be able to vote using rotary dial or pulse phones.

Voters may use the NMB's TTY communications system as explained in the Instructions. When the voter uses the TTY communications system, the voter must identify himself or herself with the correct Access Code. NMB election officials will assist the voter as necessary.

37. Q: Are TEV and Internet Voting secure?

A: Yes. The TEV and Internet Voting process requires an Access Code to vote from either medium. The use of an Access Code enhances the integrity of the TEV and Internet Voting process, and as the systems are linked, users are locked out after repeated incorrect Access Code entries.

The TEV and Internet Voting system is both secure and encrypted. The physical infrastructure for the system is housed and maintained in a locked and access-controlled facility by the Board's contractor. Elections are conducted through the contractor's facility on a continuous basis, and alerts are sent immediately to contractor personnel if any interruption to normal operation of the system is detected. All votes are received directly inside the system's firewall and are stored there.

Further, the system maintains multiple, detailed, independent audit trails which allows the contractor to substantiate election results and address election challenges.

Election results cannot be viewed until the election is closed and the tally conducted, thus eliminating the possibility of manipulation. The system is set up with various safeguards so that no one, including the Board Election Administrator, can link the content of a vote to the identity of a voter.

After the Tally

38. Q: What happens after the tally?

A: If an organization or individual receives a majority of the valid votes cast, it will be certified as the representative. If the majority of votes cast are for no representation, no representative will be certified.

39. Q: If a representation application is dismissed, does the current representative of the craft or class of employees lose its representation rights?

A: It depends. If an organization files an application for a craft or class that is already represented, the incumbent organization is a party in the investigation and election. If the organization which filed the application does not have an adequate showing of interest or for some other reason the application is dismissed prior to an election, the incumbent organization will remain the representative of the craft or class. If the investigation proceeds to an election and a majority of valid votes are cast for no representation, then the application is dismissed and the incumbent organization loses its representation status.

40. Q: What is election interference?

A: The RLA states that a carrier shall not "interfere . . . influence or coerce" its employees in the choice of representative. In order to determine whether there has been interference in the election, the NMB examines whether the "laboratory conditions" essential to representation elections have been tainted. When there are allegations of election interference, the NMB examines the "totality of the circumstances" to determine whether the laboratory conditions have been tainted. The NMB has found election interference where the carrier: conducts improper surveillance of employees; interrogates employees; discharges or disciplines employees; confers benefits on employees, and; solicits or collects ballots. The NMB has shortened the application bar period when organizations have solicited or collected ballots.

41. Q: What should an employee do if he or she observes interference during the election period but before the ballot count?

A: Except in extraordinary circumstances, the NMB will investigate allegations of interference only after the ballot count. Therefore, if an employee observes conduct which may be interference during the election process, the employee should report it to the organization conducting the campaign or to the carrier, as appropriate.

42. Q: What if the organization or the carrier believes that there was interference with the election process?

A: Written allegations of interference must be received by the NMB no later than 4 PM, Eastern Time, seven business days after the count. Responses to the allegations must be received within seven business days after the NMB receives the interference allegations. The interference allegations must state a prima facie case (evidence sufficient to establish) that laboratory conditions were tainted and must be supported by substantial evidence in the form of affidavits and documents. After receipt of the submissions, the NMB will determine if there is a prima facie case of election interference. If the NMB determines there is a prima facie case, the investigation will continue and the NMB will issue a decision. If the NMB finds interference it can order a number of actions, including a rerun election. See Manual Section 17.0 here: Representation Manual.

OTHER INFORMATION

43. Q: What if I am already represented and I am unhappy with the organization?

A: The RLA does not address relationships between employees and their unions, including the payment or amount of union dues, or the representation you receive from the union in negotiations or grievances. Some questions can be answered by the U.S. Department of Labor Office of Labor- Management Standards at www.dol.gov/olms/

44. Q: Is the NMB involved in carrier mergers?

A: In a merger, the NMB will make a determination if a "single transportation system" exists based upon an application from an incumbent organization representing a craft or class on the pre-existing or merged carrier, or from any other organization or individual. If the NMB determines a "single transportation system" exists, it may order a representation election. See Manual Section 19 at: Representation Manual (https://storage. googleapis. com/dakota-dev-content/october-2015-final-manual.pdf).

45. Q: What if there is a merger of labor organizations? Will the NMB transfer certifications?

A: Upon request of the organizations, the NMB will transfer the certifications to the new organization absent evidence of fraud or gross abuse in the merger procedures.

46. Q: If the NMB certifies an organization to represent my craft or class, do I have to join the union?

A: Under the RLA, a carrier and an organization may negotiate a "union shop agreement" which allows employees at least 60 days from the date of their actual employment to join the union or begin paying a fee to the organization, and limits the obligation to "join" to the payment of uniformly required dues and fees. This provision of the RLA preempts state right-to-work laws. Employees are permitted to become "agency fee objectors," and pay only certain fees which are "germane" to the organization's representational activities. Information on that right can be obtained from the organization. See 45 U.S.C. §152, Eleventh(c).

INDEX

A

B

C

I

J

L

M

N

O

P

Q

R

S

T

U

V

W